RIDE WESTERN

A Complete Guide to Western Horsemanship

BY LOUIS TAYLOR

e goal of Western horsemanship is to ake the horse an extension of your own ysique, so that you can move any part that extension as deftly as you move ur own body—but more swiftly and werfully. The rider must relax, move ith the horse, and constantly be aware the horse's rhythmic motions.

This book offers the most comprehen- ve treatment of Western riding avail- le, and is suited to both beginners and vanced horsemen. It will also increase e fun of the spectator at rodeos and rse shows, because it helps him under- and what he's looking at and see things was never aware of before.

The author gives a concise history of e development of Western horsemanship er the past four and a half centuries, om the early conquistadors through the a of the working cowboy with his spe- al needs, to today with its emphasis on ling for sport.

For the beginner the book explains what do with a green horse and continues ep by step through training to the fin- hed product suitable for competition or e as a personal mount. There are valu- le hints about deciding on the type of rse you need, the qualities to look for,

how to buy, and how to house him. There are tips on the posture most conducive to relaxation and safety. Discomfort for the beginner means that there is some- thing he is not doing right—and the au- thor tells you how to find out what you are doing wrong and how to overcome it. There is instruction on haltering, saddling, the first rides together.

For the experienced horseman who wants to improve and become a winner in a particular skill, *Ride Western* is a text and handbook containing secrets and methods garnered from the experience of top performers as well as from firsthand knowledge of the author. There is a great deal of material on special training and competing with the reining horse, the rope horse, the cutting horse, and the trail horse and on barrel racing and the show ring.

At the back of the book are Notes on Equipment, covering halters, bridles, sad- dles, rigging, stirrups, special equipment for bareback riding, what equipment is best for comfort, etc. The Glossary ex- plains the special terms used by the Western rider.

18 drawings by Rosemary D. Taylor, 49 photographs.

RIDE
WESTERN

A Complete Guide
to Western Horsemanship

BY LOUIS TAYLOR

Illustrations by Rosemary Taylor

Cover photograph

DEMETRIUS — 7 year Arabian gelding

Ridden by owner, riding instructress
MARY FARNELL
Sylmar, California

1975 EDITION

Published by
Melvin Powers
WILSHIRE BOOK COMPANY
12015 Sherman Road
No. Hollywood, California 91605
Telephone: (213) 875-1711

Printed by

HAL LEIGHTON PRINTING CO.
P.O. Box 1231
Beverly Hills, California 90213
Telephone: (213) 983-1105

LIBRARY OF CONGRESS CATALOG CARD NUMBER: 68-15998

ISBN 0-87980-252-9

CONTENTS

ABOUT THE AUTHOR

Louis Taylor was born in Columbus, Ohio, in 1900. Though he has degrees from Ohio State University (B.S. in Education, 1925; M.A., 1927) and has also studied at the University of Arizona, he objects violently to being called an academic horseman. He has judged horse shows in Wyoming, Montana, and Arizona, and in the 1930's left the position of trainer and manager of one of Kentucky's largest horse breeding and training establishments, Land o' Goshen, to manage the horse breeding and training operations of the LaDue Ranch at Sheridan, Montana. In 1945 he bought a small ranch of his own in Pinal County, Arizona, where he has bred and trained horses as an avocation. He presently lives and enjoys using his own horses in Scottsdale, Arizona.

A frequent contributor to horsemen's magazines, Mr. Taylor is also the author of *The Horse America Made; Ride American; Bits: Their History, Use and Misuse;* and *Out of the West.*

Louis Taylor has bred and shown horses all over the country, played polo, fox-hunted, taught equitation at several universities, been a judge at horse shows, hunted mountain lions in Arizona, punched cattle in many spots of the Southwest, and ridden trail throughout the Rockies and the Sierra Nevadas.

INTRODUCTION

"What do you mean, *Western* riding? What's so 'Western' about it?" As he said it, there was a smile on his face. I knew it was kindly, though the saber scar on the cheek next to me gave the corner of his mouth a downward turn. With the toe of a boot he pushed back a little ember that had rolled too far out onto the hearth, then took off his boots and settled deeper into the worn Morocco leather of his old chair.

My friend's life had been horses—in war and peace. Whether Tartar ponies on the Steppe, Barbs in North Africa, Walers in Australia, Thoroughbreds in Ireland, or Saddlers in Kentucky, his mounts had been the horses of lands he was led into by fortune or sent into by his government. He had used them and loved them and learned their ways. In the last year of the struggle to keep the cavalry alive in our armed forces, he was sent to the Orient to study ways of improving our remounts and our use of them. He was called home when the order for complete mechanization of the cavalry was issued.

My only reply to his question was a rather lame, "Well, that's a pretty long story."

"Is it?" he countered. "Isn't the Western seat identical with that of the rider of a deep polo saddle, or a park saddle in England? What does the Western horse have in his mouth but a duplicate of a Weymouth bit? Suppose you put a cricket in the port and cover it with a copper hood; doesn't the action of that bit remain the same as that of curb bits all over the world? Isn't your goal of perfection the same as that of your English brothers?"

"I'm not so sure," I managed. "Just what is that goal?"

At that, my friend hoisted himself out of his chair and walked over to the commodious bookshelves lining the wall opposite the fireplace. With very little searching, his hand reached a worn, red book. When he settled again in his chair, he turned quickly to a dog-eared page and read, "Complete harmony of horse and rider is the goal. When that is reached, the horse will flex with a smile and champ the bit while the rider holds the reins lightly in sensitive fingers"; and as the book closed in his lap, he queried, "Is that the goal of Western riding?"

"Well, yes, in a general sort of way," I responded.

"Do you know what kind of horsemanship it refers to?" my host asked.

"I can see by the words on the cover that it has something to do with dressage and that it was published in England," I said.

"Exactly," he replied. "So what is so unique in Western riding? About all you can point to is that Western riders use a saddle equipped with a horn."

"No," I objected. "That's not all. Western riders do many things with horses that no other American or English riders do, and they do them very skillfully. They also do many things that other kinds of riders do, but they do them a little differently. I'm going to write a book explaining all those things and also explaining where they came from and how they can be learned."

From that conversation came the book you have in your hand.

1

FOUNDATION OF
WESTERN HORSEMANSHIP

Christopher Columbus was reaping the reward usual for great givers of knowledge and insights, death in chains (in a Spanish prison). And also, as usual, his gift prompted violent action by his beneficiaries. Human activity in those days was as dependent on the horse as it is today dependent on the motor vehicle. Lust for gold, spurred by the approaching death of Columbus, caused thirteen horses and expert horsemen to land on the shores of the new world he had discovered.

These Spanish conquistadors brought to America a horsemanship in sharp contrast to the English horsemanship introduced later by the first settlers of Virginia and New England. For the Eastern colonists, the horse was little more than transportation. He was guided by lateral pulls on the reins (plow rein), and the rider hung onto the reins, sat back on his buttocks, and stuck his feet out before him.

For the Spaniards, the horse was transportation; but he was, more importantly, the tool of conquest, the extension, the magnification of his rider's physique. The conquistador moved his horse more deftly than he could move his own body. The mounted conquistador could shoot forward like an arrow at a band of awestruck Indians, stop instantly, and flash ironshod forefeet over their heads, terrorizing them into flight or submission. Today we can classify the movements of our Western reining horses—rollback, sliding stop, sidepass, quarter turn, figure eight, lead change, and so on. The movements of the conquistador's mount were too numerous to catalog.

The Spaniard rode with his feet under him. The movement of his hands on the reins was slight and subtle. A light touch of the rein on the side of the neck would spin his horse to right or left. The lightest pressure of a very certain kind would bring hocks under him and forefeet off the ground. Another would shoot mount and man backward out of harm's way.

This kind of horsemanship has a long history. The first written record of it that has come down to us in complete form is the one written by Xenophon some four hundred years before the birth of Christ. General Xenophon's cavalrymen knew nothing of horseshoes, though they knew much about how to keep hooves tough. They had no saddles, but their bareback riding was a far cry from that popular with young riders today. The bits they used were without the leverage of our curb bits, but they were composed of spiked rollers (called hedgehogs) and things much like the "crickets" seen in some Western bits. Had one of those Greek cavalrymen depended for one instant on his reins for balance, as many young bareback riders do today, his mount's mouth would have been a bloody mess—and he would probably have found himself on the ground with his horse on top of him. Perfect balance and light hands were perhaps the most obvious qualities of Xenophon's kind of horsemanship. Modern riding-school authorities might call the horse's performance "getting behind the bit." But though the Greek horses were able to get their hocks under them and flash their forefeet in the air on command, they certainly never had the habit of rearing or running backward at will as do horses that get behind the bit.

From Xenophon's use of the most authoritative bits and the lightest of hands probably comes the Western use of the slack rein. Certainly, Greek horsemanship is the grandparent of the light hands of the Spaniards. The bits the conquistadors used had no spikes, as did Xenophon's, nor were they jointed in the middle like his. However, the conquistadors' descendants, the Mexican vaqueros, who rode wild and often half-broken horses to work wild cattle, sometimes used spikes and rowels in their bits. Another Spanish departure from Xenophon's bits was the use of leverage. The Spanish bit had sidepieces, or shanks, like our modern curbs, with which the mouthpiece acts as a fulcrum and the shanks as levers, raising the chin chain or strap against the lower jaw. The Spanish sidepieces were flat and thin. They were wide just below the juncture with the mouthpiece so that they afforded no temptation to the horse to lip the bit (reach out with his lips and take the shank into his mouth). These sidepieces were usually silver-mounted and cut in intricate designs in which were crescents, stars, and other details suggesting Oriental influence. The cutout parts of the design had a very practical purpose. A sufficient amount of metal was cut out so that the bit balanced properly in the horse's mouth. This was important, because in the center of the mouthpiece was a spade or spoon, two or more inches long, with an opening at its base containing a small copper roller or two, which a horse seems to enjoy playing with. If a horse's mouth is tightly closed, the spade will act upon the roof of the mouth when the reins are pulled. However, contrary to popular opinion, the purpose is not to cause pain to the roof of the mouth, for the curb chain permits only a slight turning of the mouthpiece and a slight relaxing of the jaw immediately relieves pressure on the roof of the mouth. If the bit is properly balanced, the spade lies in the mouth with no pressure on the tongue or roof of the mouth when the reins are slack. Fairly accurate replicas of those Spanish bits are still available at better Western saddle shops. This is perhaps unfortunate, for unless a horseman has devoted his life to the kind of horsemanship brought to us by the conquistadors, his use of a spade bit will be disastrous to his horse and disappointing to himself. Any use of a spade bit on a horse not properly prepared for it by a year or so of training with a bosal (a rawhide noseband that exercises its authority on the jawbones) is folly, as the conquistadors well knew.

The old Spanish method of training a horse, preparing him for acceptance of the spade bit by prolonged use of the bosal, is beautifully described in *The Hands of Cantu*, by Tom Lea, and will be described less beautifully, but in more detail, later in this book. Briefly, the young horse was ridden with the bosal alone until he began to comprehend what was wanted of him. Then a spade bit was added to his gear, but without any use of its reins. Very gradually, slight use of the reins attached to the bit would begin to accompany use of the bosal reins. The bosal would not be abandoned until the horse was completely responsive to the bit.

According to the best account we have of the horses of the conquest (*Horses of the Conquest,* by R. B. Cunninghame Graham), Spanish equitation at the time demanded proficiency in the use of two seats, each with its appropriate saddle. One, called *a la brida,* was a direct descendant of the horsemanship of the age of chivalry—stirrups were long, the seat of the saddle was heavily padded. This was the seat the Christians used when they made their crusades to the Holy Land.

During the crusades they learned many things from the Sara-

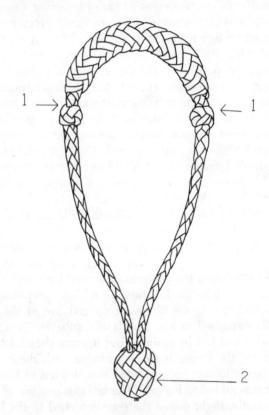

1 →

← 1

← 2

Bosal: 1. Movable buttons. 2. Heel knot.

cens, among which was a new seat on a horse. The infidels rode with short stirrups. "They had," writes Graham, "almost the appearance of kneeling on a horse's back." This suggests the modern jockey seat. However, Graham tells us that when the horse galloped, the rider of this school (*a la gineta*) stood in his stirrups and leaned back against the high cantle of his saddle. The highest praise given to a gallant cavalier was, "a man who can ride well in both saddles."

The use of the short stirrup persisted for a few years in the new world, but the conquistadors were forced to yield to circumstances and modify the saddle to a seat more suitable to circumstances—one that eventually became the cowboy's seat. It is interesting to note that though there is no indication that the conquistadors used the rope, their favorite saddles were equipped with a funny little knob, or pommel, called an apple.

2

BIRTH AND GROWTH OF

WESTERN HORSEMANSHIP

The coming of the Spanish longhorn cattle to the Californias changed the funny little knob, or apple, into a horn. The use of the *lazo* in handling the wild cattle soon necessitated stronger rigging in the saddle, but the horsemanship, the bits, and the *já-quima* did not basically change. "Tight reins and spoiled horses go together," was the belief. The hidalgo's love of grace and elegance kept alive some respect for fine gaits and beautiful movement, but practical demands soon made stopping, starting, dodging, and economy of movement the cardinal virtues of horse performance. The horsemanship that produced these virtues became Western horsemanship. The horse and horsemanship for display survived, but in a minor role.

THE SPREADING OF WESTERN HORSEMANSHIP

On April 20, 1598, Juan de Oñate crossed the Rio Grande near what is now El Paso with 80 wagons and 7,000 head of livestock, of which about 100 head were mares and colts and 700 were horses and mules. If Don Juan was not the first Western rancher, he was certainly the first of note; and it is safe to say that the seventeenth century ushered in the longhorn cattle of Mexican origin that within a little more than a century became so plentiful that they were slaughtered chiefly for their hides.

The Spanish tool for handling cattle was a long prod pole, but Mexicans raised their cattle in open country and necessity created the rope. The gauchos, some of whom were migrants from Mexico, tied their rope to the cinch of a saddle that was little more

6

than a pad; but the vaquero who migrated to Texas had adopted the war saddle with its long stirrups, hung two pieces of cowhide from the large horn (metamorphosed from the old *manzana,* or apple), which would wrap around his legs like modern chaps, and used the horn for a snubbing post for his rope. The first saddle he used was Spanish-rigged; that is, it had but one cinch, which was directly below the horn. Obviously, this would make trouble in heavy roping, so he soon added a hind cinch to keep his endgate down.

For reasons too complicated to include here (some of them tied up in the history of the missions), California cowboys developed a horsemanship that differed in several respects from that of the Texans. They stuck to the single cinch of their Mexican progenitors and adapted it for roping by putting it farther to the rear. So, today, the center fire, or three-quarter-rigged, saddle is considered a piece of California equipment. Texans developed the use of the snaffle for breaking colts and the use of the curb and short-shanked grazing bit for work stock. The Californians became masters of the fast rein and achieved it by use of the bosal and the spade of their forefathers. With the exception of these differences, early Western horsemanship was fairly uniform. The relatively long stirrup, the slack rein, the tall-in-the-saddle seat, and the practice of letting horses run free until mature before breaking them—all such things typified Western horsemanship from the Pacific to the Pecos.

Horsemanship, important though it was, was only one of many skills necessary for the survival of the Westerner in the days of the big cattle spreads, and horses were only one tool of the industry. As tools, they were expendable. There was a limit to the amount of time and work that could go into making them. This statement may seem at variance with the cry of the old-timer that modern horses are phonies because no one takes the time to make real ones, and that today we use gadgets and gimmicks to try to do in a few weeks what the old-time horsemen would take a year to do with a horse. I agree thoroughly with the old-timer. He is talking about the top cutting horses and flash-reined horses of the old West. When I speak of the limitation of time in making the tools of the trade, I have in mind the bulk of the work stock of a cattle ranch—the expendables. Unbroken horses were cheap and plentiful. The work of the range was rough and dangerous. Many horses were crippled; many were stolen by Indians and whites. Replacements were made in the quickest and easiest way possible.

When a horse was mature or nearly so (say, four or five years

A *real* working outfit—seasoned, experienced cowhands on a roundup in 1934 at the 88 Ranch in the Superstition Mountains. The white mule is representing the Craig Ranch, which used mules on its extremely rough terrain.

old), at the time of spring roundup he would be given to one of the twisters—every big ranch had one or two—to break. As soon as he was "broke," he would go into one of the strings of the working cowboys. He was considered "broke" if, alone, a waddy could rope, saddle, and fork him without committing suicide. The cowboy who got this green horse had no time to be a trainer; he had work to do, highly specialized work. He had to head off and turn wild cattle. Often he had to rope a bad one and run down the rope and hog-tie it while the rope was tied to his saddle horn. That men and horses survived such a life is a source of wonder.

Certainly, it is not strange that Western horsemanship is concerned primarily with quick starts, stops, turns, and general handiness above all else.

GRINGO INNOVATIONS

Cattle and horses spread north from California. Great cattle spreads, some backed by English capital, sprang up in Texas.

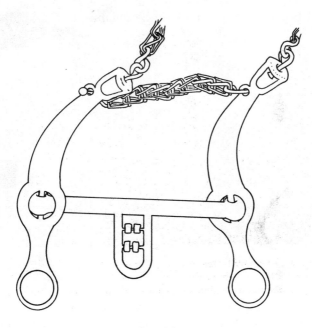

Half-breed bit.

Neither the mountain men of the northwest nor the venturesome gringos coming into Texas from the East rode with the light hand of *jáquima* and spade users of Baja California. They took from the vaquero his tools and his phrases. Being unable to use either authentically, they transformed them. The *fiador* became Theodore; *macate*, McCarty; *vaquero*, buckaroo; and *jáquima*, hackamore. The *jáquima* in the hands of a deft Mexican trainer worked on the jawbones and made a finished product so light in the

mouth that only the most subtle hands could use it. The hackamore of the northern cowboy worked on the nose to haul and pull
the cayuse around until he caught on sufficiently to be managea-
ble by a curb bit (the spade bit of the California vaquero meant
only torture to a horse "trained" with a gringo hackamore, and
the spade was rapidly replaced by the curb outside of California).

In the mid-1800's, East Coast merchants shipped some saddles
and bridles from the East to the Southwest. The saddles were

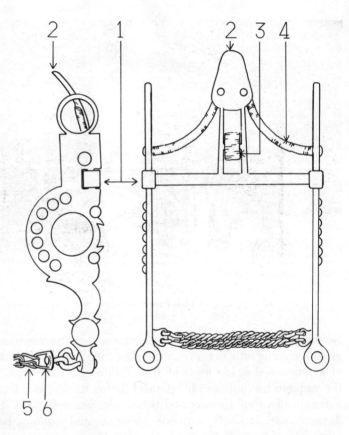

Spanish spade bit: 1. Swivel clasp. 2. Spade. 3. Copper-covered roller.
4. Copper-covered brace. 5. Chain. 6. Swivel.

useless, but perhaps they prompted the Texans to improve the old California saddles they rode. The bridles from the East undoubtedly carried some snaffle bits, for the snaffle bit gradually replaced the hackamore as the most popular training device. This gave a new direction to the evolution of Western horsemanship, so that today the Western horseman uses the best techniques handed down from the lighthanded caballeros and those descended from country squires of England, who stuck their feet

Rodeo bucker. Note flank cinch and position of rear cinch of saddle. *Photo courtesy Ben Allen, Rodeo Photos, Pasadena, California*

forward, leaned back, and hung on to the bridoon (snaffle).

The Western riding of frontier days is no more. In those days a man mounted a wild cayuse, rode the buck out of him, and then used him for the work of a cattle ranch until he broke a leg or was stolen. When that happened, as it was bound to in a season or two, a fresh bronc was easily and cheaply obtainable. Today horses are valuable, and most of them are ridden for enjoyment. Old methods of training won't produce these valuable animals. The few bronc riders alive today do not ride horses that fight in the old way. They fight harder, sometimes, because they buck under stimulus from electric prods and bucking cinches; but they buck differently. Also, the modern bronc rider doesn't ride to break a horse; he rides to cut with spurs fore and aft for a few seconds so he can win a prize.

3

HOW TO BEGIN

To argue between the advantages of learning to ride by taking lessons from a good instructor on school horses and those of learning by experience on a horse kept at home is fruitless. This chapter for the beginning rider will be addressed mainly to the enthusiast who is pursuing the latter course, for if the former method, learning by taking instruction, is chosen, the beginner should not be confused by having two masters—the riding instructor and the writer of this book. To take a few lessons from a riding master with the hope that after those few lessons you will be able to go it alone is worse than useless. If you decide to take a course of instruction, pick the best instructor available and work with him at least twice a week faithfully and as long as he deems it necessary for you to do so before you attempt to ride on your own.

A successful instructor will start you immediately using the "correct" posture—seat, position of hands and feet, and so on—of the finished rider. His reason, if you should ask for it, is that you should never form bad habits of posture. There is also another reason which he may not even admit to himself: A person spending money for riding lessons wants results. After the first few lessons, his friends and relatives who may come to observe his progress must see him looking like a horseman, not like a sack of potatoes tied in a saddle. The instructor whose beginning pupils do not look like horsemen will not stay in business long. One wonders how many competent music teachers have failed because they did not teach their pupils soon enough to play some little piece for mother or father, or whoever paid the bills.

Years of teaching riding in universities and considerable obser-

13

vation since then have convinced me that although riding masters have a point and can turn out some good horsemen if their pupils work faithfully, the beginner who learns on his own will do well to forget about some matters of correct form until he becomes acquainted with his mount, gets the feel of the horse's rhythm, and learns how to be comfortable in the saddle, if only at a walk for the first few weeks—or months, if need be.

If I could give only one brief bit of advice to a friend beginning to ride, it would be this: Never allow your horse to go faster than you can ride with comfort. (For the first few days, this may mean that he has to stand still.) Progress only as fast as you can do so with comfort. Any discomfort on a horse means that *you* are doing something wrong.

The goal you are aiming at is for the horse to be an extension of your own physique, so that you can move any part of that extension as deftly as you can move your own body at this moment—and at will, move the extension more swiftly and "powerfully." To reach this goal, you must first learn to move *with* the horse. To do so, you first learn to relax and to be constantly aware of his rhythmic motions.

Until you are well past what we might call the intermediate stage of horsemanship, the posture correct for the finished horseman aiding his horse in maximum performance is conducive to tension and rigidity. This correct posture requires a concave curve at the small of the back, the shoulders directly above or ahead of the hips, and the feet directly below the pelvis. This is not far from the position the frightened, tense, rigid beginner assumes the moment his horse takes a step faster than a walk. He may crouch forward a little farther and his feet will come back more, putting his weight off his seat and onto his inner thighs— until he tumbles off over the horse's shoulder.

The posture most conducive to relaxation (and safety) for the beginner is to sit down on the seat of the saddle with torso leaning slightly back, feet forward (instep directly below kneecap), and back straight or slightly convex at the small of the back. It is difficult for the beginner to maintain this posture, for the minute he becomes the least bit frightened he tenses, leans forward, pulls his feet back with knees out, and heels into his horse's flanks. Even when he thinks he is leaning back, his shoulders are directly above his hips. If he keeps his feet forward, he need not be told to keep the insides of his knees and upper calves in contact with his horse (an injunction that will stiffen his legs in spite of all you can do). With feet forward, the legs will have proper contact with the saddle without rigidity, unless he forces his toes out, in which event he can be told, "Stop sticking your toes out in the breeze!"

This will bring his knees into contact with the saddle without making him conscious of them and tensing his leg muscles. But

Position. Good Western seat shown by postintermediate student.

we are getting ahead of our story, for here we are talking about sitting on a horse when we don't even have a horse. Let's consider how to get one.

CHOOSING THE FIRST HORSE: AGE AND SOUNDNESS

An old, threadbare story points a most important moral in this matter of choosing a first horse. According to the story, a young lady went to the proprietor of the riding stable and said to

Posture most conducive to relaxation of beginner.

him, "Sir, I have never ridden. Have you an appropriate mount for me?"

"Indeed, yes," was the reply. "Here's a horse that has never been ridden. You and he can start out together."

As ridiculous as the story seems, the fact that most beginning horsemen start out looking for a young horse is even more ridiculous.

A valued friend of mine, Lawrence Richardson, who knew well the great horseman and rodeo star Toots Mansfield, recently said to me, "You know, Toots never liked to haul a horse under nine years old. Oh, he might take a younger one to a rodeo close to home; but if he was going to Madison Square Garden or Boston, he wanted a seasoned horse."

This remark led to the recall of others who used smooth-mouthed horses (horses over nine years old). There was Charlie Witlow's little gelding, with which he heeled in the winning team at one of the most talked-of team roping events in Phoenix some thirty years ago. That gelding was twenty-seven years old at the time. Gold Dust Maid set a trotting record that has never been equaled (taking into account the difference in harness, sulky, and shoeing then and now), and she did it in her eighteenth year. Joanna Jones was still winning five-gaited championships at nineteen. We could add to the list almost indefinitely.

Why, then, the notion that a young horse is preferable for the beginner or anyone else? First of all, to most people who can't tell two horses apart if they are the same color, a racehorse is the last word in horseflesh; and racehorses, especially those raced under saddle, are usually considered old and are retired at five or six years. This is because, being raced before they have matured (veterinarians tell us that important parts of the bony structure of a horse are cartilage until he is five), they are "broken down" (crippled) before they really come of age. Then, too, ranch horses that are carelessly ridden and poorly shod are frequently considered old at nine or ten.

Actually, a horse's age in comparison to that of a man is about treble. That is, a horse of nine years is comparable in age to a man of twenty-seven. The beginner will do well to pick a horse of at least that age. If he has any congenital weakness of leg, eye, or wind, it will have shown up by this time, in all probability. If he has had bad training, his faults will have become pretty noticeable by that time. He has learned how to get along with the human race, and he can teach many things to an attentive, intelligent beginner. And most important of all, it is more difficult for a beginner to spoil a mature horse than a colt.

"How can I be sure of a horse's age?" I am frequently asked; or, "How can I tell a horse's age by his teeth?"

At your county agent's office or from the United States Department of Agriculture you can get bulletins that explain and illustrate clearly and briefly the changes that occur in a horse's mouth indicating his age. However, if you are a beginner, a poor way to start your acquaintance with a horse is to try to stick your thumb in his mouth to force it open and hold it that way while you examine his teeth. In doing so, you will display your ineptitude and also give the impression that you are matching your knowledge against that of the dealer—a signal to him that no holds are barred. If the horse is registered in any of the recognized breed registries, his age is on his papers. If he is not a registered animal, his age can be checked by the veterinarian who examines him for soundness; and you should pay money for no horse, regardless of who is selling him, until you have employed a veterinarian to examine him for soundness. If the owner refuses to allow this, you have cause for suspicion. Look for another horse.

And while we are on the subject of papers—the proof of breeding and proper registration—here's an important word of warning. *Never* pay for a registered horse until the transfer of ownership has been recorded with and acknowledged by the association in whose book the horse is registered. The owner may quite justifiably require that you place payment in the hands of a bank or mutually trusted third party until the pedigree is cleared; but no matter how bothersome this may seem, it is very necessary to keep the cash from changing hands completely until the transfer of registry has gone through the association and is acknowledged by it. Frequently an honest owner is in error about the authenticity of a pedigree. It is possible that he is ignorant of some infringement of rules in a past transfer that makes his paper nontransferable. Of course, if the owner is actually selling a registered horse at a nonregistered price and you have no false hopes of getting papers in your name, you may be justified in closing the deal. But many a heartache has been caused by the credulity of a buyer who was assured, "If those papers don't come through, you can have your money back."

Even if the seller keeps his word, by the time the paper business is settled, the new owner has become so attached to the horse that he will not part with it.

TEMPERAMENT

Anyone with enough money can go out and buy a racehorse that will win or a show horse that will collect championships (as long as he stays sound), but finding the personal mount that suits *you* is a very difficult matter and takes time and study. Soundness, the prerequisite, can be determined by the veterinarian; but only you can determine the temperament that will make a mount suitable for you. The sensitive, high-strung person will not be happy or successful with the horse that is a bit on the sluggish side or the one that requires some manhandling; yet such a person will not get along with the highly excitable horse or one that is speed crazy. For the high-strung person, the mount often has to supply the horse sense. The rugged, "outdoor," "masterful" person will soon make the sensitive horse explode. Such a horseman will get along well with a mount with a less sensitive skin, one that can take a little roughhousing in good spirit.

A wise dealer will not allow a rider, especially an inexperienced one, to take a horse home and try it out; but he will allow the prospective buyer (or an experienced friend of the buyer) to try out the horse under his supervision. If possible, the trying out should include some riding outside an arena. Even if this is not possible, you (the inexperienced prospective buyer) can ask to see the horse load in a trailer. You can ask to see him mounted by someone carrying a slicker who will pass it over the horse's rump and across its shoulders as he is putting the raincoat on. The horse should be tied, to demonstrate his willingness to stand hitched to a rail or post. Each of its four feet should be picked up and handled.

Of course, any worn-out or sluggish horse is apt to pass all the tests just mentioned, but the horse you are looking for must pass them and also be responsive. Though he should stand still on a loose rein when asked to do so, he must instantly flex his neck and collect himself when his rider gathers the reins; and he must move out briskly on a good, fast walk the moment his rider wishes. He must respond to his rider's leg by taking a step to either side from a standstill. Without moving (or moving very slightly) his forefeet, he must respond to leg signals by moving his hindquarters to one side or the other. In a similar manner, he must be able to move the forequarters without moving his hind feet. He must back willingly a few steps when asked and stand to be mounted from either side. After a short but swift gallop, he should be willing to walk quietly, without fighting his head. If possible, ride him (or have your friend ride him) in company to be sure he has no tendency to kick other horses or to become excited when in a group.

If you can manage to see the horse loose in a corral and observe him as he is being approached and haltered, you can tell a good deal about whether or not his temperament has been spoiled by ill-treatment. If he shows signs of fear when approached from the front (becomes tense, throws up his head, and tries to dodge away), be wary of him, though a horse spoiled for being caught in the corral is not always unsafe elsewhere.

TYPE

Of all breeds prevalent in the West, the Quarter Horse is by far the most popular. If you prefer striking color, there are two separate registries for the Paint and the Pinto—breeds that look alike to the unpracticed eye, both of them good old Western types. Then there is the Palomino, for which there is a breed registry although there is some argument as to whether or not it is a breed in the sense of a group of animals of uniform characteristics capable of transmitting those characteristics to their offspring. The Appaloosa is a strain of horse cherished by the Nez Perce Indians and now gaining considerable popularity, having a breed association and a registry that is growing rapidly. It is tough, intelligent, and levelheaded. Among the horses of any of these breeds it is possible to find an excellent horse for any kind of Western riding.

Aside from the personal satisfaction of owning a registered mount, there are only two reasons for paying the difference in price between a registered animal and one without papers—first,

Western horses include types ranging from horses like those of the conquistadors to their lowly descendants, Indian ponies. The two extremely different types exchanging greetings here are native Arizonans. *Photo courtesy George Axt Photography, Covina, California*

it is easier to find a buyer for a registered animal at a fair price than for an unregistered one; second, if you have any notion of ever raising a colt from a mare you buy, a registered one is the only kind to buy, for a colt without papers is worth very little compared to a registered one until and unless he is well trained and proves himself to be an excellent performer.

If these reasons for buying a registered horse are not important to you, save the extra money and look for a good horse without papers. You can't ride the papers.

Judging type is very difficult for the inexperienced. A trusted friend who is a good judge of horseflesh is perhaps of more help in picking a first horse than is the study of books; however, here are a few pointers that are pretty important: First of all, if the horse does not have feet and legs large enough to carry his weight, don't buy him, no matter how many other virtues he may have. His legs should not be extremely long in proportion to his body and should be longer from the knees and hocks to the body than from the knees and hocks to the hooves. The distance from a point just behind the withers to the lowest point of the front cinch should be great, and his barrel should not "tuck up" at

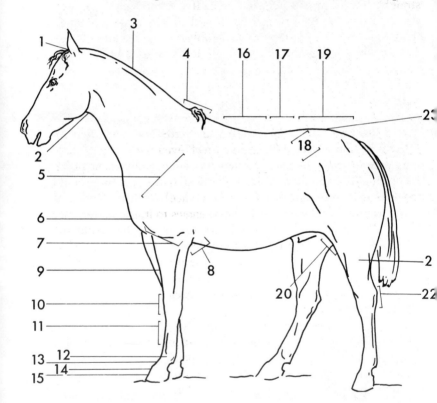

1. Poll. 2. Throat. 3. Crest. 4. Withers. 5. Shoulder. 6. Chest. 7. Arm. 8. Elbow. 9. Forearm. 10. Knee. 11. Cannon. 12. Fetlock joint, sometimes called pastern joint. 13. Pastern. 14. Coronet. 15. Hoof. 16. Back. 17. Loin. 18. Point of hip. 19. Hips. 20. Stifle. 21. Gaskin. 22. Hock. 23. Croup.

the flanks. A horse with a short back and long hips will stay fat on less feed than one with a long back and short hips. A sloping shoulder usually means an easy ride (and some other important virtues). Avoid a short, thick neck and short, stubby pasterns—and long ones that give down (become horizontal) at each stride. Viewed from the front, a good head is diamond-shaped, wide between the eyes (which are about halfway between the poll, or top of the head, and the top of the nostrils), with a fine muzzle, and with ears that are set close together.

Stand some distance from the horse and have him trotted straight toward you. Watch his feet. If the forefeet swing outward as they move forward, he is said to "paddle," or "wing." This is a fault that detracts considerably from his value, though for moderate riding outside the show ring it is not a great handicap. If his forefeet swing in toward the opposite leg as they move forward, he is said to "dish." This is a more serious fault than paddling. It may cause the horse to "interfere" (strike the opposite leg) unless he is very carefully shod. Swinging out of the hind feet is less of a fault than paddling in front. The horse that interferes behind is very difficult to correct, even with careful shoeing. Viewed from the side, the horse's action (movement of his feet) should be round, or at least elliptical, that is, his foot should move as if it were part of the rim of a wheel. Such perfection of action is rare, but the nearer the horse comes to it, the better. (By tricky shoeing, show-horse people try to imitate it.) Avoid the horse that touches the ground with his hind feet (especially at the walk) as they move forward from stride to stride. This is sometimes called "dragging behind." At the walk, as at other gaits, the feet should snap up off the ground at each step, not shuffle or slither over the ground.

As to color, remember the old saying, "No good horse has a bad color," which means that color is the least important quality of a horse; or, if he is good in all other respects, his color does not matter. As a general rule, the less a person knows about horses, the more he is likely to judge them on color.

A BRIEF WORD ABOUT QUARTERS

In *The Horse America Made*, I describe in detail the conversion of a garage and back yard into quarters for a horse; here we shall take time only to consider some of the requirements for the horse's safety and health—and your convenience.

In horse-and-buggy days, most horses were kept in a "tie stall," one about five feet wide and ten feet long with a manger at one end to which the horse was tied constantly whenever he was not in use. This did very well then, for the horse was used as frequently as the family car is today. In 1968 this will not do, for no one has the time to give the horse as much exercise as he had then. We need a box stall about twelve feet square. The floor should be well drained and of such material that his iron-shod feet will not dig holes in it. Asphalt (without a slippery surface) and what is called in the West decomposed granite are very good. Concrete (again, without slippery surface) and brick are too hard for the well-being of the horse's feet unless they are kept well covered with bedding.

The walls of the stall should be of two-inch lumber up to four or five feet high. In warm climates it is very important to arrange for the stall to be open above the five-foot level so air can circulate. The roof must not leak or be low enough for the horse to bump his head if he happens to toss it.

Mangers should be made so that they can be easily cleaned. The hay manger must be deep enough so that the horse will not toss the hay out onto the floor.

Water must be always available for the horse. A good, big bucket in a rack that will hold it firmly in place is very satisfactory. The faucet must be outside where a playful and inquisitive nose cannot reach it. Automatic waterers are good as long as they work and the horse has been taught to operate them.

Stall doors must be stout and on good strong hinges. Most important of all, there must be a provision for fastening the door open. Many a horse has been crippled—a hip knocked down—so he had to be destroyed because a stable door blew shut or swung shut as he was being led into his stall. A foolproof latch is a most important part of equipment—any smart horse can learn to operate an ordinary latch. Many a horse has walked out of his stall to death from founder on feed or from running loose on the highway because his owner was not careful about the kind of latch he put on the stall door.

Feed must be kept dry and in a place where it is impossible for the horse to get at it if he should chance to get out. A fifty-gallon metal drum is a cheap container and satisfactory if fitted with a lid a horse cannot open or rats penetrate.

A corral is a must for the horse that is used irregularly. It need not be very wide but should be long enough to give him a chance to stretch his legs. Fifty feet is a minimum length. The fence is important. It must be at least four feet high—five is better—and of such material that he cannot catch a shoe in it. The use of barbed wire around a horse is the easiest and quickest way to pain for the horse and expense for the owner that I know of. Electric fence is very useful as an adjunct to a good corral fence—to prevent wood-chewing and pawing—if it is used according to the instructions that come with any of the underwritten units on the market. But be careful; I have known of several deaths of horses kept behind homemade electric fences.

BEFORE YOU RIDE

You have a horse! Your first impulse is to climb on him and, like Don Quixote, ride off in all directions. Don't. If your new purchase is to yield you maximum return for your investment, you must become aware of him as an individual creature. Lot and lots of horse owners shortchange themselves by not doing so. For so many centuries the horse was a very important tool in man's life. As such, he was regarded as a thing, almost a machine. So in our culture there is a fixed attitude toward the horse that shuts us off from much of the possible return on an investment in a horse. Most of us enjoy the personality of a dog. We respond to him—in varying degrees. The dog helps us do this. If we are too stupid he will put a paw on us or, if we step on his toes for such conduct, wag his tail and smile. Not so the horse. He has learned his appointed place through the centuries (for many, a place of misery). By a tentative movement of an ear or flexing of a neck muscle he may try to "speak" to you; but if you fail to respond, he gets the message and will not try again. Of course, at feeding time he will paw and nicker, but these things are lyrical outbursts to which he really does not expect any response.

Go to that corral enclosing your new horse, put a halter on him (no two horses respond to haltering in the same way). Lead him about the corral. Get the feel of him. Watch what he sees and how he responds to you. If there is a bit of grass nearby that he can nibble without danger of picking up oleander-leaf fragments or Johnson grass (deadly poison under some conditions), lead him out of the corral and let him nibble the grass. If he is a bit on the playful side, you may want to put a bit in his mouth (put the bridle on) before you take him outside. If so, be careful that you don't let the reins flop down so he can get a foot over them.

Now, after you and the horse have established a little rapport, take him back into the corral or stall. Tie him (by halter, not bridle) in the corner—three feet of rope between halter and fastening—fastening at least four feet above the ground. Groom him and saddle him. Adjust the bridle so that the bit fits snugly up against the corners of his mouth and the chinstrap or chain allows the shank (sidepiece) of the bit to come to a forty-five-degree angle—no more—with the mouth when a rein is pulled. A loose chinstrap means a pinched corner of the mouth; a tight one means no leverage.

Keep your horse's head in the corner of the stall (just where it was when he was tied) for your first mounting. If he is restive, put the halter on again and tie him. Get on and off several times. Then untie him, but have his head in the corner as you mount.

Stand as close to your horse's left shoulder as you can when you mount. Of course, if you are short and he is tall, you will think this impossible. All right. Stand facing the seat of your saddle, but not back against the horse's flank. Stand close. If you stand away from the horse, you will swing into him as you rise. Furthermore, you will tend to pull your saddle off to one side.

Now grasp your reins and either the saddle horn or a good big wad of mane in your left hand. Fashion changes from year to year about whether the horn or the mane is proper, but either will do. The important thing is to hang on with that left hand. Don't let temptation lure you into letting go of the reins and horn to help your left foot into the stirrup. Using the *left* hand for this purpose is the mark of the greenhorn and the possible cause of injury and a spoiled horse. Have the reins just short enough in that left hand to feel the horse's mouth. If they are too short, you

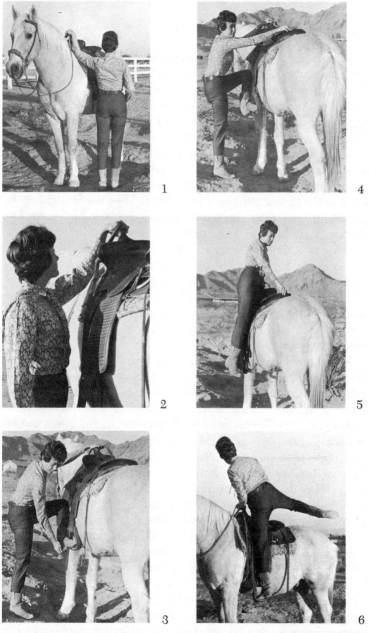

Mounting. 1. Standing close to shoulder facing croup. 2. Detail of left hand holding reins and grasping horn. 3. Using right hand to aid placement of foot in stirrup (note that the left hand maintains its position). 4. Right hand grasps cantle. 5. Rider rises to standing position, left leg straight, still facing cantle. 6. Right hand leaves cantle as right leg clears the horse's croup.

are telling him to back up, and he may respond. If they are too loose, he may take a step forward; and you won't be able to tell him that's not part of the game.

Next, put the ball of your left foot in the left stirrup. (If you put your foot too far through or if you are standing too far away from your horse, you will poke him hard with your toe as you rise. He may interpret such treatment as a signal to move to the right or straight ahead.) If you have difficulty getting your foot into the stirrup, use your right hand, *not your left*. Now, grasp the cantle of the saddle with your right hand. Then rise straight up in that stirrup, just as if you were stepping up on a high step. Do not turn your body or start to swing your right leg until your left knee is straight. Then swing your right leg over the horse's hip. Swing it high enough to avoid touching him. As your leg swings over the horse's hips, your right hand changes its grip from the cantle to the horn or swell of your saddle. Do not release the hold on the reins with your left hand until your right foot is firmly in the right stirrup. Then, and only then, are you ready to "tell" your mount to move.

The expert rider on the well-trained horse starts his mount by "collecting" it (a process to be discussed later) and squeezing slightly with his legs. The best way for the beginner is to turn the horse slightly to one side or the other, turning him back into the desired direction as soon as he starts forward. Turning him out of the corner of the stall or corral where you have mounted him is a signal for him to start. The Western horse is turned by neck rein. You simply move your bridle hand to the side toward which you wish to turn. This means that if you wish to turn to the left, your bridle hand moves to the left, bringing the right rein against the horse's neck—the signal to him to turn left. If your horse is a bit on the sluggish side and does not respond readily to the neck rein, a pull outward on the left rein (assuming you are turning left) will help the situation on this first ride.

REINS

The most obvious difference between Eastern and Western handling of the reins is that the Easterner rides hanging on to his reins (sometimes for dear life) and the Westerner rides with a

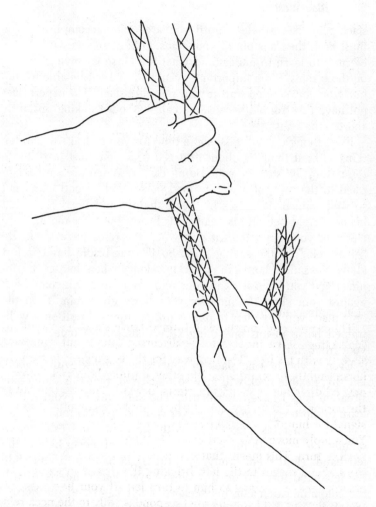

Shortening rein: Right hand behind bridle hand (left) pulls rein through bridle hand. Right hand should never touch rein between bridle hand and bridle.

slack rein. Nevertheless, until you are quite accomplished you must keep the slack out of your reins. Otherwise you will take an eternity to learn to understand what the horse is "saying" to you on those reins. More important, even, you will not be able to stop him from any sudden start if your reins are slack. The expert does not have this trouble because he can, without thinking, instantly shorten the reins.

Even though it will take some time for you to learn to shorten reins without thinking about it, it is a trick you must learn to do right from the start of your riding career. When pressure is applied to the reins of a well-trained horse—and a good many not so well trained—he raises his head slightly and bends (arches) his neck right behind his head. This brings the bit some distance closer to your hand than it was when the reins were slack. He "gives rein," as the saying goes. So if your bridle hand is just above the saddle horn (the place it belongs when you are beginning) and you have slack in your rein, your hand will come back against your chest the moment your horse gives rein. Then the only place you have left to pull is *up*. An upward pull on a well-trained horse means one thing very definitely—"Come up with your front end!"

Even if you had no slack in your reins, a horse with a good, lengthy, flexible neck will give so much rein that this dangerous situation is as I have described it. The only way to avoid it is to learn to shorten your rein whenever your horse gives rein.

To shorten reins, grasp them with the right hand (still maintaining the hold with the left hand) a couple of inches behind the left hand. Hold them firmly with this right-hand grip and slide the left hand forward on the reins. Never, *never,* interfere with the communication line between your left hand and the horse's mouth by using your right hand in front of your left one. An expert rider can shorten reins without having the tension on those reins vary even the smallest fraction of an ounce while they are being shortened.

As soon as you have started your horse out in the direction you wish to travel, be sure you do not have more pressure on the reins than just enough to take out the slack. More than that will mean to your horse that you want him to walk just as slowly as he possibly can, or to stop. If you are sure you are not slowing your mount down with your reins and he is doing a very slow and sluggish walk, bring your heels into his sides to tell him that you wish him to walk out. If he takes one step faster than a walk, restrain him with a pull on the reins; but be sure to *release that pull the instant he returns to a walk. Never* allow your horse to do any gait that is uncomfortable for you. Discomfort means that you are doing something wrong, usually because you are trying some movement for which you are not yet ready. Your learning will progress much faster if you heed this warning. If you disregard it, you may very probably develop certain patterns of rigidity which you will never be able to correct. I have seen show-ring judges who have been fooled by the uncomfortable rider, but a good judge is not fooled by such a rider.

SEAT

Eventually you will be able, when occasion demands, to ride up off the seat of your jeans and on your inner thighs, with your insteps directly below your hipbones, your shoulders leading, and your back concave. But if you attempt this posture at first, you will develop habits of rigidity hard to overcome. Keep your feet (heels level with insteps or slightly lower) forward, with your legs dropping straight down from the knees, the insides of your knees and upper thighs in relaxed contact with the saddle, your torso leaning slightly back. All this means that your weight will be on the seat of your jeans, as it is when sitting in a chair. Ride at the walk, and only at the walk, until you can do so comfortably with a relaxed waist. It is your waist that takes up the difference between the rhythmic movement of your horse and the steady progression of your torso. Your bridle hand should be relaxed and steady, not reflecting the movement of your body. If it moves at all, it should move with the movement of your horse's head, not your body.

BEYOND THE WALK

It is best to avoid riding in company, or at least all company other than very sympathetic and patient friends, until you have become so comfortable at the walk that you are ready for faster gaits. When you *are* ready, try only a few steps at a very slow trot at first. Relax in your waist and lean back. Keep your reins short enough so you can stop the horse the moment you become uncomfortable. When you jog some distance in comfort, try posting. This must be done at a little faster trot than the jog you have been sitting comfortably.

The trot is a two-beat gait—two-four time. Listen to it and count it as your horse jogs very slowly with you. Now stop your horse. Let him stand still while you count, "One, two; one, two; one, two," etc. On the count of one, sit down with your weight on the seat of the saddle and on your inner thighs, but lean well forward, with your shoulders a few inches ahead of your hips. On the count of two, rock forward, using your knees as a pivot, and put your weight on your stirrups. In doing so, the seat of your jeans should rise above the saddle a few inches. Count steadily and continue rocking until you can do so smoothly and evenly.

Now let your horse move out on a trot faster than the jog you have been sitting still on. Count his strides, and rock with your counting. If you rise at just the right height for the particular horse you are riding and lean forward at the proper angle, you will find that the horse helps you so much that posting is as effortless as rocking in a rocking chair. If you get a double bounce as you come down into the saddle (the fault of most beginners), one of four things is wrong: (1) you may not be counting exactly with the impacts of the hooves on the ground; (2) you are rising too high; (3) you are not rising high enough; or (4) you are not leaning forward far enough.

You should do your posting in a corral or an arena until you can do it easily and until you have mastered that most difficult part of posting, the proper use of your hands. The corral or arena is a must, because only there will your horse be willing to trot steadily without increasing his speed beyond the limit of safety and be willing to stop at any time.

Proper use of the hands is important for safety's sake and for the sake of your horse's mouth. It also quickly distinguishes the greenhorn from the rider. As you rock forward and back in posting, your bridle hand tends to move in rhythm with your body. Even if you think your hand is still, it is very probably not. Test it by sticking your little finger down until it touches the saddle horn very lightly. See if you can steadily maintain this light touch. The trot is the only gait this test will work on because it is the only gait in which the horse's head is steady. At the walk and at the gallop (lope and canter) there is rhythmic movement of the horse's head which the bridle hand must follow. Though the bridle hand is the one that gives most of the trouble in posting, some practice is needed to get the right hand to function smoothly in shortening rein while posting.

Do not attempt to ride your horse at a rapid trot outside a corral or arena until you can post well and use your hands deftly while doing so.

THE LOPE

As described elsewhere in this book, the lope and the other gaits of the same hoofbeat pattern (canter and gallop) are three-beat gaits—done in three-four time. They are done in two "leads." Here is the sequence of hoof impacts with the ground at the left lead: (1) right hind; (2) left hind and right fore simultaneously; (3) left fore. Here is the sequence of the right lead: (1) left hind; (2) right hind and left fore simultaneously; (3) right fore. The forefoot that works alone rises slightly higher than the one that hits the ground simultaneously with the diagonal hind foot. This foot that works alone and rises higher is called the leading foot. If it is the right foot, the horse is said to be on the right lead. If you are on top of him and have become an experienced rider, you can observe the right shoulder moving farther forward than does the left one. This business of leads seems quite complicated at first. Don't bother about it until you have learned to sit comfortably on the lope. When you do learn about the leads, you will wonder why they once seemed so baffling and complicated.

The horse with a good lope moves like a rocking horse in the nursery. Sit on him just as you did on that hobby horse. Remember? With your waist muscles you kept him at his furious pace back and forth. The same works on the real, live horse with the exception that it takes less effort. Lean back, keep your feet well forward, and use your waist to keep him rocking. The feet also help keep him rocking by their rhythmic pressure on the stirrups.

That's why it is easier to ride the lope with the ball of your feet on the stirrups than it is with your feet clear through the stirrups; your flexing ankles have a chance to get into the act, making pressure on the stirrups increase and decrease in rhythm with the up-and-down movement of your horse's head.

Because at the lope your body is steady, leaning back easily until you have become quite accomplished, your bridle hand will not be the problem it was at the trot. However, at all gaits see that your hand goes with the horse's mouth, not with your body. Also, at all gaits keep the reins short enough so that you can instantly restrain the horse if he starts to go faster than you can ride with comfort. This is especially important at the lope, because to get him into that first lope you tried, you had to push him fast enough on the trot to get him to break into a gallop. When he did that, you probably had to pull him down a little to get him into that good slow lope, didn't you? The slower he lopes, the easier the ride. Just keep enough pressure on the reins to keep him from gaining speed.

ENJOY YOURSELF

Until you can sit back and enjoy your horse out in the open, you will not be ready to try advanced riding. Do most of your posting, if you prefer, at home in the corral, but see some country from the back of a good horse. When he walks, jogs, and lopes, relax. When you ride with friends who are learning to ride the forward-seat way and you seem to detect some criticism in their eye for your violations of the rules they are trying to follow, just take a good look at them. Don't they look somewhat like stiff, stuffed monkeys bouncing along? When you are ready to get forward on your horse, you will be able to do so without the painful stage they are in.

4

ADVANCED WESTERN RIDING

After you have ridden sufficiently to feel comfortable and secure at all the movements of your horse and can communicate with him to some degree, you are ready for more ambitious riding. We may think of advanced riding in two categories: (1) show-ring competition and (2) the more strenuous riding done today in a more or less stylized version of what was once the reason for the existence of the horseman of the West—fast running, barrel racing, roping, cutting, and using the horse for transportation over the long trail. Let us begin by considering the first category, show riding.

Any statement of the perfect position of the Western rider, or any other kind of rider, is misleading. It carries the suggestion of a static, fixed position, and overattention to it at the outset is likely to lead to rigidity. Of course, the opposite—constant shifting about in the saddle or constant movement of the body—is as bad or worse. With this calculated risk of error kept well in mind, let us consider the very hypothetical perfect Western seat.

Viewed from the left side, the back of the rider's heel appears directly below the center of his hip joint. The back of his elbow is directly above his hip joint. The center of his shoulder is directly above that. What a terribly rigid picture! However, this is the point of departure and the standard for judging the seat. The view from the rider's right side is identical except for the position of the elbow. Show-ring fashions change rapidly and radically for Western riding because Western riding has been accepted in horse shows only within the last thirty years or so, and its standards are not extremely well established. Because of all this, the position of the rider's right arm is a seasonal matter. The last word I had on the matter (from a competent judge late in 1966) indicated that the right elbow could be slightly behind the position of the left elbow, a rather bad thing because it tends to aggravate the fault of carrying the left shoulder ahead of the right one. However, it does facilitate ease in following another current dictate of fashion—at present (1967–1968)—that of grasping the romel (a long, braided rawhide attached to the reins) a few inches below the bridle hand and carrying the right hand below and behind the bridle hand.

Let us now consider another perpendicular line of relationships from the side view. The back of the rider's knee should be directly below his belt buckle, unless the rider is very obese or pregnant. This obviously answers the question "How long should the stirrup leathers be?" for if the leathers are too short, the knee will be too far forward; and if they are too long, the knee will be too far to the rear. In the show ring, the rider's bridle hand (the left one) will be carried a few inches ahead of his body and just high enough so that the reins will clear the saddle horn. This is a very dangerous position of the bridle hand for any but the accomplished horseman, because the moment the horse raises his head a trifle or brings his chin in (which he will do at any slight signal to increase speed or move forward from a standstill), he will give the rider several inches of rein. Then the rider will lose contact with his horse, because a novice cannot instantly shorten rein,* and he has not enough room between his bridle hand and his body to allow him to pull back on his reins as the horse's head comes up or his chin comes in. The rider's alternative, of course, is to raise his hand high in the air. This is a signal to his horse to rear or jump forward. So, all but the most accomplished horsemen *must* carry the bridle hand just above and slightly ahead of the horn. I have asked several respected show-ring judges how much a rider is discounted for holding his bridle hand ahead of his saddle horn. The consensus was, no discount at all in equitation classes in which there is an age

---

* To shorten reins, as we've said, the right hand grasps the reins immediately *behind* the bridle hand. The bridle hand then slides forward on the reins.

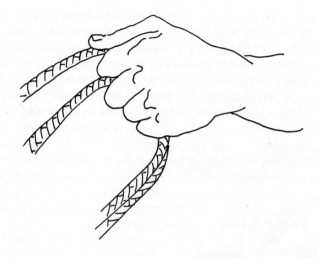

Single rein in one hand for neck-reining—one acceptable method of holding reins.

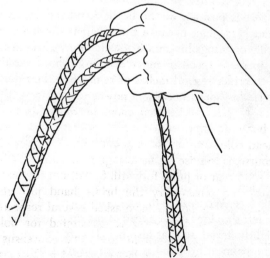

Single rein in one hand for neck-reining, sometimes called the roper's hold.

limit and none in others unless the competition is very close. Carrying the hand ahead of the horn may, of course, cause the elbow to be carried forward. This, too, the judges say, is permissible; but the shoulders must be even.

Let us now view our hypothetical perfect rider from the rear. His spine is perpendicularly in line with his horse's spine. He is in contact with saddle leather from his crotch to the center of the

Correct posture viewed from the rear.

inside of the calves of his legs (no daylight between knees and saddle). His toes are turned very slightly outward; the bottoms of his boot heels are lower than his stirrups.

A front view of our hypothetical rider reveals, first of all, a smile on his face. We can see that he is not "leading with his left"; that is, the left shoulder is not ahead of his right shoulder. His left wrist is slightly flexed, so that his knuckles are toward his horse's ears and the palm of his hand is toward his own body. The reins are held lightly but firmly. If our rider is in the show ring, he holds the reins in the currently fashionable manner. In 1968 this is with no fingers between the reins.

Both elbows are, of course, close to his sides, with the arms

One of the accepted placements of hands in Western pleasure-horse classes (1967).

hanging relaxed from the shoulder. His right hand holds his romel or the ends of his reins several inches below his bridle hand, and it lies relaxed upon his thigh.

CORRECT START

Before asking the horse to start, the rider should collect himself into the saddle position outlined above. Then he should simultaneously put enough pressure on the reins and leg squeeze on the horse to get at least a very slight flexing of the neck just behind his ears, and some muscle tension or movement of the horse's quarters. If he is mounted on a sluggish or poorly trained horse that will not flex at the poll or respond to a light squeeze of the rider's legs, the pressure on the reins will have to be accompanied by a very definite neck rein to make the horse move a forefoot in preparation for a turn (as prescribed for the beginner in the foregoing chapter); and the squeeze of the legs must be transformed into a very definite kick.

With the well-trained horse, the rein pressure and the leg squeeze will result in "collection"; that is, the horse will begin to mouth the bit gently and move his hind legs to get more of his weight on his haunches. Then all the rider has to do to execute a good walk is lessen slightly the pressure on the reins. His position at the walk is the one he has already assumed.

The sluggish or poorly schooled horse which has to be started at the walk by turning one step to right or left must be immediately returned to the desired direction as soon as he starts to walk, and the rider's problem from then on is to maintain just the right pressure on the reins to keep the horse looking alive and enough impulsion from the spur, heel, or leg to keep him moving.

Spurs are not a necessity in Western riding, and they should never be used by the beginning rider or by any rider to inflict pain. With most horses, the accomplished rider finds spurs are an advantage to both himself and his horse, for a touch with the spur is much more definite than a touch of the heel. Even though he is equipped with spurs, the accomplished rider uses only the leg squeeze to start his horse at the walk. It is important for any rider to know how to give this aid, the leg squeeze. It is given with the

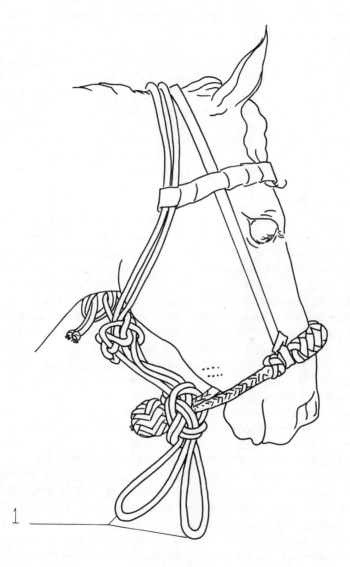

1 _____

Hackamore with fiador (theodore). Reins fasten at 1.

middle or lower part of the inner calf of the leg. When the inexperienced employ it, they sometimes move the knee outward away from the horse, showing daylight between horse and the inside of the leg just below the knee. This is the mark of the greenhorn. Don't do it. As we shall see later, use of this pressure, or aid; by one leg only is very important for certain purposes, but the first use is of both legs for the squeeze to start the walk. When pressure of only one leg is used, the beginner sometimes raises his heel as he squeezes. He is especially likely to do so if he thrusts his knee out. If he does this while wearing spurs, the bad habit will be quickly broken, for a raising of the heel and a squeeze at the same time will bring the spur into the horse's side. Always keep heels down when using the leg aid.

THE JOG

A generation ago, one of the most successful commercial horsemen, well known in Kentucky and Missouri, had the slogan, "No trot, no horse." If he were active in his business today, he would have to revise his slogan; for the trot as he knew it is not one of the gaits of the Western horse. It is true that now and then one sees an exceptional Western horse that can be made to swing out on a good trot with round action, but that gait is not considered an asset by the Western rider. I have seen Western show classes in which the judge called for a walk, jog, *trot,* and lope (on rare occasions, miscalled a canter). But such judges would not have given a second look at any horse that did what saddle horsemen a generation ago called a trot. What the modern Western judge wants when he calls for a trot is a diagonal gait a little faster than a jog. He wants neither the action nor the reach formerly demanded in that gait in the show ring, though he requires just enough speed to make sitting the "trot" very difficult for amateur horsemen. Because he does so, posting is now considered proper by most Western judges when they ask for a "trot." This inclusion of the trot and the propriety of posting (considered by some Western judges an important necessity) are still debated matters among professional Western horsemen and judges, so the rider who wants to be "correct" in the show ring or elsewhere will do well if he finds out from local authorities exactly what the current fashion is before he displays his horsemanship at the trot.

In its broadest sense, the term "trot" designates any diagonal gait, that is, any gait in which the off fore and near hind hoofs strike the ground simultaneously (or so nearly so that the ordinary eye or ear assumes simultaneity), and the near fore and off hind hoofs, of course, also act simultaneously. With this in mind, we can say that the jog is a very slow trot, one just faster than a walk. While the well-trained Western horse starts the lope from a standstill and could probably do the same with the jog, it is customary to use the walk as the starting point from which any other gait is taken. The propriety of going from a trot directly into a lope is maintained to be an exception to this rule by some horsemen; and not infrequently, a show-ring judge will ask for such a performance. However, until the rider is extremely accomplished and his horse well trained, it is advisable to use the walk as the starting point for each other gait and to return to a walk before changing gaits.

So, let us consider show-ring etiquette in starting the jog from the walk. To do so, the rider raises his hand slightly and squeezes with his legs (uses leg aid). If he overdoes this on the well-trained horse, the animal will lope instead of jog. Therefore, it may take practice to determine the exact amount of rein pressure and leg aid necessary to produce the desired result. As the aids are given (rein pressure, like leg pressure, is considered one of the "aids"), the rider's body is inclined *very* slightly forward and he puts a *little* more of his weight in the stirrups than is used in the walk (which was approximately his weight from the hips down). All movements of the rider in changing from walk to jog should be as slight as possible. Such movements in the show ring by a good horseman are so slight that they are rarely observed in the grandstand.

All riding is a matter of balance, and the horse is kept in the jog by being balanced between the restraint of the reins and the impulsion of the legs. This does not mean that the rider constantly squeezes with his legs (or flails with his heels).

As soon as a horse responds to the aids by starting forward, his rider should release the rein pressure sufficiently to give as much slack in the reins (or to come as close to giving slack as possible)

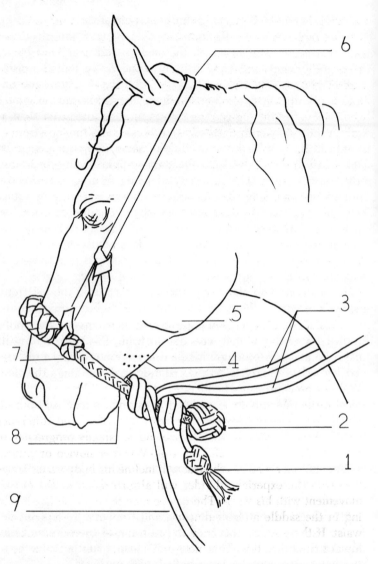

Simple hackamore: 1. Rope tassel. 2. Heel knot. 3. Reins. 4. Point of pressure when reins are pulled. 5. Cheek. 6. Whang leather. 7. Button. 8. Chin. 9. Lead rope.

as he can without increasing speed. In the show ring the Western horse is judged on his ability to "work on a slack rein." This phraseology is a bit confusing to the novice, for it does not mean that the rider gives up all contact with his horse's mouth. The slack of the reins is sometimes almost imperceptible, and the flexed fingers and wrist of the rider very subtly move in rhythm with the horse's head. The slightest shift in the slack of the reins gets instant response from the well-trained Western mount.

The body angle at the jog is inclined *very* slightly forward from the perpendicular. The inexperienced rider whose waist is rigid will necessarily have to put too much weight in his stirrups and absorb the motion of the horse by flexing his ankles. The accomplished rider absorbs with his waist the difference between the rhythmic following of his horse from the waist down and the steady progression of his body from the waist up. In other words, from the waist down, the rider moves in rhythm with the jogging horse; from the waist up, his body moves steadily forward.

THE TROT

Because the change from jog to trot is a change in speed, not a change in gait, it is not necessary to bring the horse to a walk before making the change. All that is needed is a slight increase in the slack of the reins. If the horse is a bit on the sluggish side, a little leg pressure may also be needed.

As in the jog, the novice rider, whose waist is stiff, will put his weight on his stirrups and take with his ankles the difference between the movement of the horse and the steady progression of his own body when he sits the trot. Whether novice or professional, the rider who sits the trot will incline his body very slightly forward. The experienced rider will absorb much of the horse's movement with his waist. The novice may try to do so by slouching in the saddle and bending his spine toward the rear at the waist. If there is any tendency to bend at the waist, it should be toward the front, though at no instant at the trot is the spine at the waist static when an experienced rider sits it.

As mentioned in the foregoing chapter, there is no complete uniformity in requirements in Western classes in shows. In most Western shows in 1968, posting is required at the trot in Western

pleasure classes. In some Eastern shows, possibly because East-
erners want to be sure their Western classes are "real Western,"
riders must sit the trot. If posting is required in a class in which
you are competing, you must do it correctly, easily, and grace-
fully and be able to use the proper diagonal; so let us consider
posting as it should be done by the advanced rider.

Horses vary greatly in the way they move at the trot. On a
horse with very low action and a short stride, the rider's body
when posting, inclines very little more forward than when sitting
a trot. However, if the horse has good round action and a fair
stride, the rider's body, when posting, will incline forward until
his shoulders are directly above his knees. Good posting is effortless for the rider. He rises no higher than the impetus of each
alternate stride of the horse sends him. On the short-gaited, low-
going horse, the rider carries a little more of his weight on the
stirrups than at the jog, and his rise at each alternate hoofbeat is
barely perceptible. With the horse possessed of good round action and fair stride, the posting rider will sit well down in the
saddle at each alternate hoofbeat; and on the other hoofbeat, the
horse will give him a very definite rise. In proper posting on a
horse with a good trot, the rider rocks on his knees. His hip
joint oscillates very little. If the hip joint acts as the hinge, the
rider will pop up and down like a jack-in-the-box. The posting
rider's feet should remain still, with heels well down, not rising
and dropping as the rider posts.

The posting rider's shoulders move forward and upward as one
forefoot (and the diagonal hind foot) rises. Therefore, if the
rider's shoulder moves forward and up with the left forefoot of
the horse, we say he is posting on the left diagonal. His weight is
on the stirrups as the horse's left forefoot is at the top of its stride,
and the rider's weight is on the saddle when the horse's left forefoot is on the ground. When you are mounted, it may be difficult
to see that forefoot, but you can watch the shoulder. It moves
forward as the foot comes up.

It is required in the show ring that you post on the left diagonal when going to the left around the ring, and on the right
diagonal when going to the right. In other words, you rise out of
the saddle with the rise of the horse's forefoot nearer the outside

of the ring. Only veteran riders are able to start with the proper diagonal at the horse's first step at the trot. So when you ask your horse to trot, start with him by posting easily on either diagonal. If you find that you are posting on the wrong one after the horse is settled in his gait, shift to the other diagonal. Here is the way to do so:

When your weight is off the stirrups (you have just rocked back onto the seat of your saddle), break the rhythm of your posting by sitting the next stride of your horse and rising on the stride that follows it. A beginner once explained it to me this way: "You sit just one bump and rise on the next one."

I have seen some comical results (and one tumble) when students tried to shift diagonals when their weight was on their stirrups; that is, staying up on their stirrups for an extra beat instead of sitting the extra beat.

The ultimate test of your posting and your ability to change diagonals is your own comfort. If you are comfortable, the chances are pretty good that you are graceful.

The lope of the Western horse is little more than a very slow gallop. It is not the highly collected (weight on the haunches) gait properly called a canter in three-gaited or Eastern pleasure classes in horse shows. However, now and then a judge in a Western class will call for a "canter" when what he means is the good old Western lope. Such a judge would probably be shocked if a horse appearing before him would at the request "Canter" get its hocks well under its body and rock along on a true canter.

Whether we call the gait we are considering a canter or a lope, this is the way you should ride it in the show ring.* Keep your heels slightly lower than the balls of your feet, and your feet directly below your pelvis. The insides of your knees and upper calves should be in contact with the saddle. If they are, your toes will be pointed correctly—slightly outward. If your knees allow daylight to show between them and the saddle, the backs of your calves will contact the saddle and your toes will turn out. This will put you out of competition.

---

* This is *not* the method prescribed for the beginner in Chapter 3, and should not be attempted until the rider has completely learned to keep his body relaxed properly and in rhythm with the movement of his mount.

Your weight is carried almost equally on your upper, inner thighs and your stirrups. Your torso should lean slightly forward, with shoulders square and at right angles to your horse's backbone, avoiding the fault of leading with one shoulder, described above. Arms and hands at the canter should be as described earlier in explanation of the hypothetical perfect Western seat.

As the horse moves along at an easy, slow lope on a slack rein, your ankles must be flexible to enable you to keep rhythmic pressure in the stirrups. In that rhythm, stirrup pressure increases as the horse's head moves down in his stride and decreases as his head moves up. There is also rhythmic tension and relaxation of the muscles of your waist, so that from the waist down you rock with the horse, keeping constant your contact with the saddle, while from the waist up your torso moves steadily forward—no bobbing back and forth or up and down.

Western classes require that a horse must lope (and do other things too) on a slack rein. This does not require that you have a foot of loose rein to haul in whenever you want to slacken speed. It means that you are riding with no tension on the reins. When you return to a walk from the lope, put enough tension on the reins and apply enough leg aid to collect your mount. This may mean that you have to shorten rein to avoid raising your hand. Do so as deftly as possible and see that your right hand is at its proper place, as described earlier.

Always have your horse comfortably collected when making any turns the officials in the ring may require. When you are asked to back your horse, respond immediately but not in a jerky or hasty manner. Collect your horse and back him straight for the few steps required. (The judge will signal you that he is satisfied as soon as your horse takes a very few backward steps.)

Every moment you are in the ring, you are demonstrating to the judge or judges. Unless you are in an equitation class (in which *your* ability is what counts), it is the horse that is being judged, and you must see to it that he is showing every moment. When you are lined up after having demonstrated all the movements required, don't let your horse "sit down" on one hind foot or otherwise indicate that he is done with this show business.

In any class, equitation or other, keep your attention on your demonstration to the judge, not on your friends at the ringside or in the ring. Keep your horse as much of the time as possible where the judge or judges can see him. This means that in a very large class, as many Western pleasure classes are, you will not continually ride as close to the rail as possible. On the other hand, the rider who continually cuts the circle small in order to keep closer to the judge than other horses will irritate even the most even-tempered official.

After the awards are made, if you are not among the winners, don't rush out of the ring and don't let your horse slop out looking like a rejected lover. He is a show horse until he is out of that gate. If you are a winner, you may be asked to circle the ring. If so, comply at the most attractive gait your horse has, and hold him to it as if you were still competing.

5

TRAINING—OLD STYLE

In the old days of the big cattle outfits and the great trail drives, the methods of preparing horses for use were suited to the needs of the day. Those needs no longer exist, and a horse educated ("broke" and "busted" were the names for the process) by that old method would certainly not be a suitable mount in today's horseback activities. However, there is an aura of glamour about each activity of those early days of the cattle industry in the West; and bronc busting has more than its share.

In our rodeos today we see a highly stylized version of bronc riding. True, today's rodeo horse probably bucks harder than the average bronc of the early days—or at least he continues to put on performance after performance, while the average bronc of the old days, usually gave up the fight after the first few saddles. Of course, he would "break in two" when first forked on a frosty morning or at some inconvenient moment of fast range work now and then, but such lyric outbursts were usually short-lived after his first few saddles. Today's rodeo bucker is the product of severe screening, which only the toughest and most persistent buckers survive. Then, too, the rodeo bucker has the added incentive of a flank cinch to keep him bucking as long as his saddle remains on his back. In some instances, the flank cinch is twisted or knotted to increase discomfort. (The flank cinch of the rodeo horse is not to be confused with the hind cinch of a double-rigged saddle. The latter is kept far enough forward on the horse's rib cage to avoid discomfort; it is kept there by a spacer, a strap a few inches long attached to the center of the front cinch and to the center of the hind cinch. The flank cinch or bucking cinch is not attached to the front cinch. It goes under the soft part of the horse's belly just in front of his hind legs.) Whether the horse is harder or easier to ride when a flank cinch is added to his gear is a question that has never been settled, though the horses on which such gear is used are the ones that have found their way into the rodeo because of their ability to buck hard and long.

The original skill, of which rodeo bronc riding is a stylized version, rose out of a necessity of the time. The need was for a way of preparing a horse for a specific use as quickly and as cheaply as possible. Raw material (unbroken horses) was relatively cheap. The finished product was not expected to be very valuable—say, twenty to thirty-five dollars. The finished product was to be used by a rider to whom violence was a natural part of daily life. The method was relatively simple—though certainly so difficult that on most large ranches it was turned over to a specialist, or several of them.

Details of the method varied widely, for men of the early West were individualists. However, there were four common factors evident in the practice of horse breaking throughout the early West. First, the horse to be broken was at least four years old. Second, he was roped, tied sufficiently to enable his tormentors to saddle and bridle and mount him; third, he was ridden under spur and quirt until he quit bucking and lined out in a run. Fourth, the process was repeated daily, with diminution of force as the horse's fighting diminished—until the rider could mount the animal without struggle, control the direction of his forward movement, and regulate his speed. Then he was considered "green broke" and ready to go to work on the range, though he might still buck a little on occasion.

The young horse might be one from a wild bunch trapped or caught on the open range. Or he might be one grown in a semiwild state on the range of the outfit where he was destined to be used. If he was grown by the outfit, his only contact with humans was in being roped, branded, and castrated when he was a yearling.

ROPING

The green bronc either was roped by the neck and choked down or was forefooted. With either method, the roping was done when the horse was confined in a corral, usually with a bunch of other horses. If the method used was roping by the neck, the rope was snubbed to a post as soon as possible after the animal was roped. As the rope tightened on his neck, his wind would, of course, be shut off. When he would plunge forward, skill was required to keep the slack out of the rope, so that he would not break his neck as he hit the end of the rope again. Gradually the horse would hang back on the rope, occasionally fighting by pawing and tossing himself from side to side. Finally, he would be choked sufficiently to fall flat on his side. Then he would be quickly hog-tied (all four feet tied together) and a hackamore would be put on his head (the halters we use today were not available in local hardware stores in those days).

SADDLING AND MOUNTING

Methods of saddling varied, depending chiefly on the amount of help available. The horse, snubbed to a post by the hackamore rope or held by several strong hands, would usually be blind-folded. He might be hobbled (forelegs tied together) and have one hind leg tied up to a rope around his neck just ahead of the shoulders. If help was plentiful, one stout hand on each side of the horse would grab and twist an ear, hanging on hard until the horse was saddled and mounted.

If the bronc buster was without help, he would use hobbles and tying up of a hind leg as the occasion demanded. The blind-fold he used might be an extra-wide brow band so attached to the hackamore that he could raise it above the horse's eyes after he was mounted.

Some busters objected to neck roping. They claimed there was too much danger of pulling the horse's neck down (a pulling of the muscles and ligaments of the neck, so that the horse was never afterward able to raise his head sufficiently to be useful). This did sometimes happen. They also claimed that when a horse was forefooted, he was easier to hog-tie and handle, for the fall, properly executed when a horse is forefooted, takes some of the fight out of him. Of course, if a roper missed and caught only one foreleg, there was a good chance that the horse would break a leg. Then, too, if a roper lacked skill in flipping the forelegs sidewise toward him at just the right split second to make the horse fall good and clean on his side, there was danger of breaking a shoulder. However, many good men who worked alone found forefooting by far the better method. After letting a horse to his feet and attaching a hackamore, they could rope the forelegs again and the horse would stand still, giving the roper time to hobble him. Some ropers could rope the forelegs and give the rope a flip that would put a half-hitch around the legs to serve as a hobble.

Both methods of roping broncs are fully explained and illustrated in Fay Ward's *The Cowboy at Work*.* Mr. Ward is writing and drawing from firsthand observation and is therefore discussing more recent times than I am here concerned with; however, the method is identical with that of earlier days.

GEAR

The cowboy of the days of the great cattle drives used what gear he could make or trade for. He could not run to a tack shop to get needed equipment as we can today. Even if it had been possible, his meager wages (even as late as 1930, a hand's wages were forty dollars per month) would have prevented buying much gear. A cowboy's saddle was usually worth several times what his horse would bring.

Much of his equipment was made of rawhide, for obvious reasons. The hackamore was perhaps the most ingenious of his rawhide gear, and certainly, a very important item. Today there is considerable discussion pro and con about the use of a hackamore in horse training, much of it prompted by fad and fashion. Seldom do we realize why the old-time cowboy used it, why he dared not put a bit in the mouth of the green bronc. We even have very little curiosity about the use of a halter on bucking broncs in rodeos, though I have heard the erroneous explanation that they are used to give the bronc a better fighting chance than he would have if a bit were put in his mouth—which may be true as far as it goes.

The bronc buster used a hackamore because a bit in a fighting

* Fay Ward, *The Cowboy at Work* (New York: Hastings House, 1958).

bronc's mouth is a great danger to the rider. One accidental pull on a bit at the wrong time will throw a fighting bronc over backward or on his side, though it is true enough that no bit is severe enough and no arm strong enough to get a horse's head out from between his forelegs, once he has bogged it and started real, serious bucking.

The hackamore used in the Southwest was a very simple affair. It was a nose band of either rawhide or hair rope held in place just above the soft part of the nose. Under the jaw, it hung low, just above the chin. The nose band was held in place by a leather strap (latigo), fastened at each side of the nose band (bosal) as far forward as possible without touching the horse's eyes. A hair rope was used as reins. Frequently, a part of the rope, which was attached to the heel (back part) of the nose band was tied around the horse's neck just behind his ears so that the nose band would not slip off under the horse's chin in the event of an accidental forward pull on the hair rope. (This and other uses of the hackamore are fully explained and illustrated in my *Out of the West*.)

The hackamore of the Northwest was usually of rawhide, a somewhat coarser affair than the bosal of the Southwest. While the Southwestern bosal was just loose enough to avoid discomfort to the horse when the reins were slack, the nose band of the Northwest was very loose. It was kept in place by what was originally called a "fiador" but later became known by the more gringo name "theodore." It was a rather elaborate affair of small rope that went around the neck, through a brow band of rawhide or leather, and was attached with some fancy knots and twists to the rear of the nose band.

On all ranches where the horse was little more than a tool of the business of handling cattle, a bit—usually a curb called a "grazing bit" (one with a bent or S-shaped shank of moderate length)—was used on the horse as soon as he was "green broke." When there was time, some cowboys used a snaffle on young horses thought to be particularly good. The snaffle was used until the horse learned to guide and to come to a stop reasonably well.

In the extreme Southwest, where the pride of the *caballero* in his mount still persisted, a spade bit was hung in the green horse's mouth as soon as he was "bucked out." He was ridden with two sets of reins, one attached to the bosal and one to the bit. The bit reins were not used until the young horse was reining and stopping well. The bit was not used to inflict pain; this was done by the bosal. It was just tight enough so that a pull on the hair-rope reins would make the bosal work on the lower jaw. If the rider needed to inflict pain, he could easily take some hair and hide off the jaw with the bosal. The only discomfort that could be caused by the hackamore of the Northwest was whatever a strong arm could do by exerting pressure on the nose. The hackamore was too loose to affect the jaw. Those few cowboys who used the loose hackamore after the rough-bronc stage (and their modern descendants) might wrap the nose band in front with wire, or even barbed wire, to make it more painful.

The finest equestrian skill ever brought to the shores of North America was that of the Spaniards, so well depicted in Tom Lea's *The Hands of Cantu*. This early Spanish horsemanship, in my opinion, far surpassed, in both subtlety and range, the best dressage and the best forward-seat horsemanship that came to our eastern shores from Europe. However, this fine Spanish horsemanship was a skill possessed only by the very few. The bulk of the horse handling on the large ranches of the Southwest was a very cruel and painful version of it. A common practice, which persisted in remote places so long that I have witnessed it, was to teach a horse to rein by throwing him and bruising one side of his crest with repeated blows of a rock or hammer. Then the horse was rolled over on his other side so that the process could be completed. The next day, when the neck was really sore, the teaching of response to the pressure of the rein on the neck would begin. There were other techniques, no more humane, employed to teach the horse to ground-tie, to stop, and to work a rope.

The other parts of the cattle country had perhaps fewer practices of refined cruelty because gringo cowboys demanded less refined performance from their mounts than did the vaqueros. However, they did need a horse that would work a rope, and one method of teaching him to do so was rather violent. A particularly wild and stout bovine would be roped with a reata or good stout rope tied hard and fast to the saddle horn. As soon as the critter was roped, the cowboy would step off and let the two animals come to whatever agreement they could. By the time the fight was over, the horse was either a very good one at working a rope or he was so badly crippled that he had to be destroyed.

6

TRAINING—BASIC

MODERN METHOD

Though much of the best part of old-time horsemanship is included in methods seen on modern ranches, there are striking differences between the old and the new ranch horsemanship. Few ranches today allow their colts to run without feeling the touch of human hands, except for branding and castrating, until they are four or five years old, as was the practice in the old days. Most modern ranches halter-break their yearlings and teach them to lead. Most start saddling at three years, some even at two.

There are several reasons for this. There is no cheap supply of good unbroken horses today. The poorest unbroken three-year-old today will often bring as much for canning (for dog and cat food) as a well-trained horse would bring in the early days of the West. Fewer horses are used on ranches today, and those that are used must be better trained than in the old days. Wages are higher today and hands must have good mounts to enable them to get their work done efficiently and quickly. Even though wages are higher, most modern ranch hands are not eager to risk their necks on half-broken horses. They are not as fond of violence as their predecessors.

Furthermore, most ranches of any size are breeding their own horses and trying to breed good ones. Many have a good Quarter-Horse stallion or two. The colts must be handled with some care, and injury must be avoided if possible. Most yearlings can be haltered by two stout and competent men without the necessity of forefooting or choking down. When the animal is deemed old enough for saddling, whether at two or three years, he can be haltered and tied. Then he is "sacked out." This means that a man very carefully and quietly approaches the forequarters of the horse when it is tied to a stout post or corral fence. In one hand he has a saddle blanket or burlap sack. He first quietly touches the horse on the shoulder or neck with his free hand. If the colt is extremely "broncy" and strikes with his forefeet, he may have to be hobbled before the sacking can proceed. Very carefully, the colt is rubbed or wiped about the head, neck, and shoulders with the blanket or sack. Gradually the sack is used farther back. Before the process is ended, the young horse has discovered that the sack is harmless, and he will stand quietly and allow it to be swung under his belly, around his hind legs, and any other place the handler desires. Proper sacking out requires great skill and patience on the part of the trainer. Any quick movement or haste on his part will make the process do more harm than good.

I once saw a well-intentioned bystander ruin a half-hour's work of a good trainer by bursting into a loud guffaw of laughter when a colt that was being sacked out stamped its foot smartly at the sack. A wise trainer allows no onlookers when he is sacking out a colt.

THE FIRST SADDLE

After a green mount has been properly sacked out, he is not terrified by a saddle, though he must be approached by the handler with skill and care when he first carries the saddle to the youngster. Both blanket and saddle must be put on quietly, usually after due inspection by the colt, both with his eyes and nose. The cinch is pulled up very gently and only just tight enough to keep the saddle from slipping back.

The length of time required to reach the stage of putting on the first saddle varies with the individual horse. Some require much time to get over their fear of human hands and contraptions. Such animals may have to be sacked out several days before being approached with a saddle. Others can be saddled immediately after a rather brief sacking out.

Procedure after the first saddle is put on varies greatly from ranch to ranch. One method is to put a hackamore on the colt or to put a snaffle bit in his mouth. Then the reins are put around the saddle horn and knotted just long enough to avoid pressure when the colt's head is in a "normal" position, that is, the position it is carried in when the colt is walking about in freedom. Reins are short enough to prevent the colt from putting his head to the ground. He is then allowed to walk about in a corral as he wishes. Usually several colts are doing so in the same corral. Company keeps them moving about and also has a calming effect. I know of one ranch that includes a quiet older horse or two in the bunch to set a good example of decorum.

On some ranches the colt's head is sometimes tied to his tail, so that any progress he makes must be circular. Such practice is usually reserved for the wilder colts. Some ranch horsemen tie the stirrups up so that they will not flop and frighten the colt when he first starts to move about with a saddle on his back. Others let them flop, and if the colt bucks a little, he soon calms down and accepts the flopping stirrups as part of the nature of things.

On ranches where time is not at an extreme premium or where the colts are considered to be of greater value than time, a transition step between the first saddling and mounting is employed. This consists of securely tying on a sack partly filled with whatever material is handy to supply a little bulk and a weight of about fifty pounds. The weight is evenly distributed on each side of the saddle.

Extremely careful ranchers make the first mounting of the young horse a very quiet affair, quite different from the old days of "bucking 'em out." Sometimes complete mounting is not done at the first trial. The colt is merely shown that a foot in the stirrup and a little weight put on one side of the saddle is a harmless business. At the first mounting, the colt may not be asked to move at all. If he does move about the corral (where all early riding is done), he is kept at a walk and guided very gently by a snaffle or a hackamore.

The variations from the methods I have just mentioned would fill a book larger than this one. Some ranches still use the blindfold on first mounting, and even on first saddling. Others use hobbles. Some tie up a foreleg, and others tie up a hind leg. However, in this day of high wages and relatively high prices for horses, many ranches use careful methods similar to those I have described.

EARLY RIDING

Most ranch-raised colts get their first riding in a corral. Ideally, this is a round corral made of heavy poles or railroad ties slanted slightly outward. The outward slant tends to protect the rider's knees when the colt travels close to the fence. It also tends to prevent knocked-down hips when colts are milling about. Cattle ranches, however, are chiefly concerned with cattle, not the ideal conditions for training horses; so the best holding corral, whatever its construction, is usually the place of first riding of green colts. There the colt is ridden until he gets some notion of what a bit is for. When he responds to the bit by turning or stopping as his rider wishes, instead of resisting and twisting his head about, he is taken out into the open country.

There is another method, used so infrequently that it merits only brief mention here. It is the use of a snubbing horse or lead horse mounted by a skillful assistant. I have seen wise old horses used for this purpose who could do much to teach a colt. When I was pressed for time in training a band of hotly bred colts raised on open mountain range in Montana in the 1930's, I used this method on the LaDue Ranch on the Beaverhead. That operation is described in detail and illustrated in Chapter 7 of my book *Out of the West*. A word of warning is in order here. If the lead horse or his rider is inept, this method can be quite dangerous and certainly will do more harm than good.

BITS

The use of the hackamore for first riding of young horses comes from the early Spanish horsemanship. Most modern use of this gear, however, is quite different from the original method. The loose hackamore with fiador is usual. This puts all authority on the nose and is much less deft and quick than the Spanish use of the bosal, which is just loose enough to release jaw pressure when the reins are slack. With a loose hackamore, the colt can be, and usually is, taught to respond to a lateral pull on the reins for direction. He is turned first one way, then another (not in too rapid succession), learning to lead with the leg on the inside of the turn before he is taken out of the corral. He can even be taught a little about stopping at this stage.

Before the youngster is taken out for work in open country, it is usual to put a snaffle bit in his mouth. Frequently a short rope or strap is fastened to the rings of the snaffle. It goes under the jaw and is long enough so that it exerts no pull on the rings, but it is short enough to prevent a ring from pulling into the mouth when a hard sidewise pull is exerted on the reins.

There is little agreement on the proper time to start exerting pressure on the neck in conjunction with the sidewise pull on the reins in preparation for teaching the neck rein. Some ranch horsemen start neck pressure at the hackamore stage; others wait until the transition from snaffle bit to curb bit. Most ranchers know that putting a good rein on a horse is a matter of time, and they do it so gradually that neither the horse nor the rider is acutely aware of the transition from plowline to neck rein.

The most promising young horses, as soon as they work well on a snaffle, are introduced to a mild curb. At about this stage the promising youngster is turned over to a competent man who has charge of a part of the range. He uses the colt to pack salt (transported by mules, led or driven), to tend pumps or windmills, to keep siphons running, or to bring in injured animals or administer first aid to them on the range. This gives the young horse his first experience in real work. Gradually he learns something about directing the movement of a cow and is introduced to a rope. On the George Taylor ranch, which, in the 1930's, stretched from the Pinal County line (Arizona) above Superior to Magma on the Southern Pacific in the Gila Valley, I have seen good young horses kept at this preliminary work for a year or even two. One of the best hands on that ranch, Chico Harquis, quietly called for his wages and quit the outfit when Wayne Taylor, his boss, insisted on taking and putting into hard work a young horse Chico had been using in his job of taking care of part of the ranch. Chico insisted the horse was not yet ready for the serious work Wayne intended to give him.

Many a young horse had received his education from Chico. Every one of them, when Chico pronounced it ready for use, had an excellent rein, knew how to work a rope, was fearless and quiet in any situation, would stand when the reins were dropped, and could do a fair job of very quietly cutting an animal out of a herd. This meant that Chico had used the youngster for at least a year, and possibly two years, in the general work of overseeing a part of the range. When asked about the expenditure of such amount of time in making a horse, Chico might reply, "Time ain't too important to a horse."

Such deliberation is, of course, an extreme. A drift fence divided the Taylor mountain range from that of another large spread whose owners had financial interests in rodeo production. Taylor did not like to hire hands who had any interest in rodeo if he could avoid doing so. The neighboring spread was manned very largely by men who had a very real interest in the great sport. The handling of horses on that range was almost at the opposite extreme from the method I have just described. Of course, the general attitude and method of handling horses was indicative of the method of handling cattle, and the practical result of this struck me forcefully one hot afternoon in the mid-1930's.

On this occasion I was with some Taylor men. Our job had been to gather some cattle on the highest part of the range and bring them down to the shipping corrals, where certain calves would be prepared for shipment to feeding pens in the valley. The neighboring ranch was engaged in a similar job. The route of both bunches (probably about eighty head in each) lay for some distance on either side of the drift fence. The Taylor cattle looked none the worse for being bunched and put on the trail, but the cattle on the other side of the fence looked as if they had been through a major battle. They were skinned up in various places. Some had an injured eye and some a broken horn. All were gaunt. How many hundred pounds of beef had been run off, I cannot guess, but the amount was large. The horses showed similar signs of battle, and they were as gaunt as the cattle. All this made clear to me the practical justification of Chico's attitude and method. On that afternoon I witnessed two extremes of horsemanship and of range work, both still to be seen on ranches of the West.

CONTRASTS BETWEEN THE OLD AND NEW

The earliest Western horse breaking was a matter of making very cheap unbroken horses into mounts for men who took violence in their stride. As soon as the horse was deemed suitable for any purpose on the range, he was put to work. If under that work he eventually showed any sign of unusual ability, such as cow sense in cutting or roping, he was encouraged. If he developed and didn't break a leg or fall into the hands of marauding Indians, he became a top horse.

As the West became more "civilized" and some of the ranges were fenced with "bobbed" wire, good horseflesh became a little more valuable. Cowhands became a little more exacting in the kind of mounts they used. The unbroken horse was given a chance to find out something about humans and their peculiar demands before he was mounted. When mounted, he was not spurred until he "had the buck out of him" and then clobbered into yielding to the rein. Instead he was allowed to get used to the saddle, get a few of the kinks out of his back, and get the feel of a hackamore or snaffle bit before he was mounted. True enough, there was no pampering of the green horse, and force was used if he did not fall into line quickly. Perhaps the outstanding virtue of this period of Western horsemanship was its use of time in perfecting the horse that showed promise. A good one might be ridden on a hackamore for a year or more, doing easy work while he learned the nature of work with cattle, developed a good rein, and learned to work a rope.

Today conditions and methods are so different from previous ones in the West that if one of the old waddies of yesterday should come back from Boot Hill and look upon them, he would not be able to believe his eyes or ears. First of all, there is more horse activity in urban and suburban areas than on the ranges. Second, a good unbroken young horse is worth many times what a top mount would bring in the old days, and only the good ones are worth the modern high expense of training. Furthermore, the finished horse today, with the exception of the relatively few still at work on ranches, is the mount of a person who lives in a modern house, spends much of his time in an automobile, and makes his or her living by doing something inside a building, usually equipped with elevators and convenient drinking fountains—to say nothing of air-conditioning. Of course, the most expensive of today's mounts earn their oats by competing in show-ring classes that last about fifteen minutes, or they compete in roping or cutting contests, which are a little more strenuous but certainly nothing like the long hours and hard work of the old days.

Perhaps one of the most remarkable differences between today and yesterday in the Western horse business is that today the marketable horse must be absolutely foolproof and tractable the moment the trainer's work with him is completed. He must be foolproof when at the peak of his physical development, or even before. In the old days the only horse deemed safe for anyone not bred on the range was an old, worn-out cowpony or pack horse.

A horse that experiences the psychic traumas incident to the old-time method of horse breaking is rarely foolproof. He may be docile enough when he is "worked down," but give him a little rest and feed and he can be triggered into the old reactions. He will break in two or buck for no reason that his rider can fathom. This statement is at variance with the ideas of many old-timers, who feel that the old-time horse of the open range was just a natural bucker and that if the buck didn't come out of him at the breaking, it would come out later. This idea has been demonstrated to be erroneous by numerous horsemen, from John Rarey in the last century to the writer of these words in the present one. However, the old-timers' ideas have this much basis in fact: the horse broken in the old, violent way came through his "training" familiar with rough use of spur and bridle. His rider's movements, often quick, and rough, did not surprise him. I am sure that if one of today's top winners of Western events could be placed on a range under an old-time waddy who would give the critter a jab in the shoulder to turn him for a dash after a dogie that had broken loose from the herd, that top horse would give that waddy about all the ride he could handle. Of course, if that top horse had been through the hands of one of the second-rate trainers who use everything from sawed-off icepicks and tacks in boot toes to "make" a show horse quickly, the jab in the shoulder might be old hat to that horse and he wouldn't buck; but it wouldn't be long before our old-time waddy would do something else that would set him off and make him break in two.

Today's riders are not the waddies of yesterday. Many of them are young and feminine. Some are men who have always loved horses and have finally made enough money to own some good ones and to learn to ride them. Today's horses, we say, are "better bred," which means that records are kept of their lineage. (Whether the blood is better than the Andalusian and Barb blood of the old-timers is open to debate.) Working conditions and the highly stylized kind of work done by horses today is different from the conditions of work in the days of cowboys and Indians; and so, necessarily, is training different.

One old horseman whose word I respect says that what a colt learns about humans the first months of his life stays with him. One learned educator once said, "Give me a child until it is seven, and the devil may have him after that," meaning that if for the first seven years of his life the child was properly educated, no evil influence could harm him later.

While there are plenty of things that can be (and frequently are) done to ruin a colt after he is weaned, early handling certainly is more important than is generally recognized. It establishes his feeling toward humans, sets his reaction pattern in response to anything a human being does with him. A colt that has been properly handled from the day he was foaled and is not mishandled thereafter is likely to have a good disposition regardless of congenital factors. I mean the kind of disposition that will enable him to give satisfactory service to a modern rider—one who frequently knows much less than the horse he is riding.

There is a widespread belief among horsemen that a pet colt is hard to break, hard to train. The belief is well founded. Most colts raised in a back yard by inexperienced people are spoiled pets. They are as disagreeable as are many of the children of today, willful, boisterous at all the wrong times, and destructive, lacking regard for anything that is said or done to them. People who have such pets colts seem to think anything the little creature does is delightful and amusing. They laugh at and encourage all he does. I have seen such people encourage the colt or even tease him to make him react in some silly way.

In spite of the incorrigibility of most pet colts, it is possible to gain a colt's confidence and affection without spoiling it. To do so, the handler must always avoid frightening the little fellow and have continually in mind the fact that it is better to avoid the start of a fight than it is to win one. I have found that the earliest stage of training is the one in which intelligent firmness is most necessary. Nevertheless, I am irritated by the horseman who says, "Never let him get away with anything!" The highly bred, well-fed adult horse has his off days. He also, if he is a real joy to his rider, has his desire to play now and then. Of course, you can beat the play out of him. If you are good enough at it, he will learn to give you a machinelike performance. If you are not good enough, he will become sour and a fighter. However, the little colt must learn that there are some things a good equine simply does not do and some things he has to do whether he likes them or not. There comes a time in the lives of most (perhaps not all) children when a wise father replies to, "Why do I hafta do that?" with, "Because I say so, and I'm bigger than you are, so get going!"

Always have a rope long enough so that you can allow the little fellow to play some, but when the serious business of leading up with his shoulder next to your hip commences (granting that you have quietly and by proper stages taught him what is required), the monkey business must end.

The best way to avoid a fight about haltering the first time is to start early. A healthy foal can be haltered as soon as he gets his sea legs under him, usually in a few minutes after he hits the ground. If the handler is present at the foaling, he will, by the time the colt is steady on its legs (sometimes this is immediately), have had his hands on the little fellow. This avoids fear of the touch of human hands. If, as usually happens, the mare foals in the middle of the night when no one is with her, the first touch of human hands must be very gentle. When the foal is nursing is a good time to start, or when the mare is nuzzling her baby. Soon it will be possible to put one arm around the front of the chest and another around the buttocks and guide the baby in a direction it wants to go anyway.

THE FIRST HALTER

As soon as the little fellow can be handled calmly, a light halter can be slipped on. Most colts are so constructed that when their heads are raised, the crownpiece of the halter slips back on the neck so far that when the head is put down to the ground the nosepiece and the crownpiece pull uncomfortably. To avoid this, a brow band must be added to the halter. I usually use a doubled strip of muslin. It will easily tear if the halter is left on for any length of time and the baby rubs his head and catches the brow band on something.

A foal's attention span, like that of a human tot, is very short, so the first attempt at leading should be of very short duration. A few turns around the stall or corral is enough. If a helper is at hand, he can provide impulsion by an arm behind the baby's buttocks; if no helper is around, the handler can hold the lead shank (very close to the halter) in his left hand and a soft cotton rope looped around the baby's buttocks in his right.

A foal should be led with its shoulder against the leg of its handler, never strung out behind like a toy on a string being pulled by a child. Of course, the first lesson will be a matter of "steady by spurts" unless much successful work has been done in handling the baby without a halter. Even so, too much rigidity at the first lessons will start a fight and set up an attitude toward humans that will be difficult to overcome. Whether he knows it or not, the trainer at this stage of the game is doing much to establish the kind of reaction the animal will have at maturity to the reins—the kind of a mouth he will have.

Of course, the pulling rider can make a pulling horse out of any animal, and a bad hand on a halter shank can make a puller out of a little foal. The hand should not pull; it should be a thing of passive resistance, like a post.

The following account of the use of the first halter training as a foundation for a good mouth is taken from Chapter 23 of my *Bits: Their History, Use and Misuse:*

In my right hand (acting as one post), over the baby's loins, I hold the ends of a loop of rope that goes behind his stifles. In my left hand (also a post that moves with him) I hold a light shank close to his halter. The first move is his. Later he can learn to start when the post starts and stop when it stops. The move may be immediate or it may take several minutes [even many minutes in rare cases]. The posts do not move until he does. Then they move just fast enough to allow him to walk briskly or trot slowly. At this first move, they may even allow for a pretty brisk rate of speed for a spurt, because I don't want to start a fight if I can avoid it. If there is one, the hands (posts) do not pull or yank, they merely resist passively.

There may be, probably will be, a few little cavorts and kicks necessitating some readjustment of the loop, but soon the baby, far superior in intelligence to his human brother of like age, will get the hang of the arrangement and will take quite a few steps in a more or less orderly fashion. That's enough. I do not want to tax his little patience the first day.

As soon as the baby and I have established an agreement about this walking with me at his shoulder, I tie the loose end of the halter shank to the side of his halter opposite me. So I have a pair of reins instead of a shank. I leave a long end of shank hanging from the new knot, and it serves as a sort of emergency shank held in my left post [hand] in addition to the rein. I hold rein and emergency shank about midway between poll and withers several inches above the tiny neck.

Now the left post (hand) occasionally moves to one side—right side for right turn, left side for left turn—and the baby soon responds to neckreining.

FURTHER GROUNDWORK

Professional horsemen, men who make their living by working with horses, cannot spend the amount of time that ideal training requires. If they did, the training bill against an individual horse would be well up into thousands of dollars. However, the owner of one or a very few horses gets his compensation from handling those horses and seeing them grow into the kind of mounts he wants. He can take the time to do an ideal job. He will be wise to avoid the shortcuts that many trainers are forced to resort to.

No time spent by an intelligent handler in leading the little foal is wasted. Obviously, the little fellow will resent being taken very far from Mama. The wise trainer will not start a fight on this score. Keep Mama close at hand when leading Baby to visit the neighbors or strolling about home grounds. By lengthening the ropes (always keeping one good long one in hand as an emergency lead rope), Baby can, after he has learned to lead up well and neck rein, be led by the handler mounted on Mama.

In a suburban area north of Scottsdale, Arizona, a rather typical American horsey neighborhood, a frequent sight is a rider or two, one mounted on a mare with foal running loose at her side or cavorting around the party. When such practice does not interfere with other riders on the trail and does not damage property, it is a harmless source of enjoyment for the owner and affords exercise for the colt. However, such practices should be supplemented by frequent leading of the colt beside the mare. He should learn to lead up beside her just as he leads beside a person on foot. Use of neck rein is a great convenience in keeping the little fellow where he belongs, and it certainly is a great help in his future education. Of course if Mama is a silly old fool, spoiled by some previous owner, a companion on a sensible horse may ride alongside and do the leading. *The foal should learn to lead from either side.*

The number of things done by amateurs and professionals to teach the colt to do what he is told and do it cheerfully before he is big enough to be mounted would fill two books the size of this one. Most young equines (about the same proportion as among young humans) like to learn. Of course this liking can be quickly squashed by the use of force on the part of a handler who does not have sense enough to communicate to the youngster what is wanted. The new should be presented in terms of the familiar; and each new step should be small and gradual. Any sign of confusion on the part of the youngster is a sign of error on the part of the handler.

It is regrettable that one very important part of a horse's education is so often neglected when he is a tiny foal. I refer here to teaching the animal to back on signal. When the foal is small, it is relatively easy to teach him to back on signal and to teach him to back straight. If the horse is not taught to back before he is mature and has learned many other things, the teaching is often not a simple matter. Many a horse has had his mouth spoiled and his disposition ruined by an exasperated rider's attempts to make him back for the first time.

As a prelude to learning to back, the foal should learn to stand still on signal for a few moments. Always remember that a tiny horse, like a tiny human, has a very short attention span, so it is not reasonable to ask a well-bred foal to stand for a very long time.

After your foal has learned what you want when you ask him

to stand still, you can begin to teach him to back. Stand directly in front of him and grasp the halter shank close to the halter. Give him the voice signal and pull backward on the halter. If he does not respond immediately by taking a backward step, put your thigh or hip against his chest and force him to take one step backward. Then pet him and get his mind off the immediate problem by walking him about for a few moments. Then stop him, let him stand for a few seconds, and again back him one step. Do not do this too many times in one lesson, but repeat this asking for one step for several days until he begins to associate the voice signal and the backward pull on the halter with the taking of one backward step.

Obviously, after he has made the association of the voice and halter signal with a step backward, it will be easy to increase the one step to two steps and then to more. When he has learned to take a few backward steps, you should begin to give attention to the straightness of his backing. With your left hand on the shank close to the halter and your right hand on the baby's hips, it will be easy to keep him backing the few steps you ask for in a straight line. Never be in a hurry in this business. Make progress slowly. Never ask him to back more then eight or ten steps, and certainly not that many until he will back willingly.

THE LUNGE LINE (OR LONGE LINE)

The two most common practices in working with the horse not old enough to be ridden are lunging and longlining. The former, often called "longeing," is the more common, though not necessarily the more useful. We shall consider it first.

Few horsemen agree on what is best to put on a colt's head when he is being worked on a lunge line. The cavesson used in the old cavalry school at Fort Riley is considered by some as the only proper equipment. It was made of several thicknesses of good leather, was provided with divided cheekpieces that would keep it in place, and had a ring in the front and one on each side, as well as the conventional one under the chin. Its devotees were (and many still are) under the belief that the only proper place to fasten a lunge line is a ring in the front of the cavesson. There is some basis for this belief (though not enough to make a fuss about), for a deft hand can, with a flip of the lunge line, stop a fairly fractious animal in its tracks if it is wearing one of those old cavessons. Also, a flip of the line fastened under the chin tends to throw the horse's head up, while the flip when the line is attached to the nose tends to keep the head down—sometimes. The old army cavesson is good if the trainer uses a dumb jockey, manu-

Cavalry-style lunging cavesson.

factured or improvised, because the rings on the sides are handy
for side reins and the one under the chin for a tiedown. However,
a good dumb jockey should be provided with an overcheck to
keep the animal from lowering its head; and this calls for a bit in
the mouth.

In my own experience with the lunge line, I can see very little
difference in the effect of a good cavesson, a fiador, or a rope
halter. The variety of human on the other end of the rope is far
more important than the variety of the headgear on the horse. Of
course, the lunge line is never (as far as one can say *never* about
anything concerning a horse) attached to a bit.

The line itself may be of webbing or of *cotton* rope at least a
half-inch in diameter. Before any attempt is made to attach it to
an equine, the handler should learn well how to coil a rope in
either hand so he can play out the coils easily and take them up
as deftly. This is the same technique the calf or steer roper uses.
Let's start with the left hand. The twenty- or thirty-foot rope
should terminate in a swivel snap at one end and a good turk's-
head knot at the other. To hold it in the left hand, extend the left
hand palm up. The knot end of the rope should cross the palm
and the knot should lie just outside the base of the little finger
(some good trainers let it drop down between the little and
third fingers). The rope thus crossing the palm leads out of the
hand at the base of the thumb. To coil the rope, the right hand
reaches out, palm up, under the rope with thumb pointing to
the right, toward the snap end of the rope, slides along the rope
to a point about three feet from the left hand, and grasps the
rope. Then, still with palm upward and thumb pointing to the
right, the right hand brings the grasped rope back to within a few
inches of the left hand. Then the left hand, still palm up with
rope end crossing it and the thumb toward the right hand, takes
the rope behind the right hand so that the rope crosses the left
palm just ahead of the end already in the hand. This will make a
loop about a foot in diameter, which the left hand quickly can
release when necessary; but the knot at the heel of the palm can
be firmly grasped so that the rope cannot be jerked out of the
hand.

The entire rope can be coiled by repeating the process I have just described for the first loop, but each loop must be added to the handful so that it can be released without disturbing what remains in the hand. Just a slight relaxing of the thumb will release a coil when the trick is learned. Of course, to hold the rope in the other hand, as is necessary when the horse's direction is reversed, the jobs of the hands must be switched.

If webbing is used for the lunge line, it can be folded neatly and a fold let out at a time—a much easier process than coiling rope by a novice. However, the weight of the rope is an advantage when flipped for a signal.

STARTING THE COLT ON THE LINE

A circular corral is ideal for lunge work, a square one almost as good. If no corral is available, the colt must be led in a circle of about sixty feet in diameter for many days until he is well aware that he is to travel that circle. When the colt is familiar with being led around the corral close to the fence or when he has formed the habit of walking in a prescribed circle in the open, start walking farther away from him as he goes in the accustomed path. At first keep him at arm's length by using your free hand to push his shoulder. Then soon, just a little flip of the rope or web line will keep him where he belongs. Very gradually you can keep him on his proper path while you describe a smaller circle nearer and nearer the center of the ring.

If plenty of patience is used, this method will work on the great majority of fairly well-bred and well-fed animals. If, however, the animal is a bit on the sluggish side and patient trial of the method just described doesn't work, or the colt continues to crowd in toward the center in spite of flips on the rope, or he stops the moment you step away from him, there are two other methods to use. The first employs the use of the whip, a tool that is capable of being used for a great deal of harm but occasionally, in the right hands, one that can be used to advantage. For this early work, I prefer a long buggy whip to a lunging whip or a coaching whip (frequently used for lunging). If the whip with a lash (lunging or coaching whip) is used, the lash should be kept wrapped around the stock and secured by tape for this early use. The butt end of the whip is used to push on the colt's shoulder to

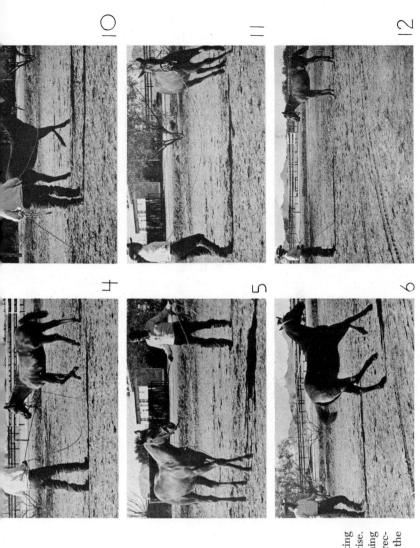

On the lunge line. Plates 1–6: Starting colt and working counterclockwise. Plates 7–9: Stopping colt and coming to center. Plate 10: Reversing direction. Plate 11: Working colt to the right. Plate 12: Stopping colt.

keep him from coming in toward the center. If he is the kind that stops as soon as you move away from him, the other end of the whip can be used to touch him behind the stifles to provide impulsion. It may be necessary to touch him rather smartly to get results, but the light, quiet touch should be tried first and then increased until results are obtained. If the colt reacts to this method by kicking or by rushing forward in a small circle around you, the method to try next is the longline.

Longlines can be of soft cotton rope a half-inch in diameter. They should be long enough to allow the driver to walk at least ten feet behind the animal. If possible, they should run from either side of the halter or cavesson through rings of a surcingle on either side of the barrel of the colt. A pony saddle or racing saddle with stirrups shortened so that they fall midway of the barrel and tie under the belly or to the girth will serve very well if the reins are run through the stirrups. However, it is possible to use the longline without such equipment, allowing them to run free from the halter to the driver's hands. In such cases, care must be taken to keep the hands low enough to prevent the lines from slipping up over the hips if the colt twists his rump to the side.

To start the colt on the longlines, lead him into the ring as usual. Start around the ring to the left, using the left longline as a halter shank and having the right one come across the colt's withers. (The ends of the lines should, of course, be coiled neatly and carried in the left hand, which is also holding the "shank.") If the colt has been taught to neck-rein, so that the reins can be carried in one hand above his withers, so much the better. Keep the colt moving around the circle counterclockwise and gradually walk farther and farther toward his rear. Of course, the lines will have to be gradually lengthened. If the colt tends to stop or slow down, a hand on his rump should keep him going, with a sharp pat or two if needed. As you work toward the rear, you can begin to use the right rein to keep the colt in the path he should follow, if necessary. When you finally succeed in keeping the colt walking in the path (circle) he is accustomed to while you walk some ten feet behind him with a longline in either hand, you can keep him moving ahead by the flip of a line (or lines) against his stifles. If he wants to trot out a few steps, don't restrain him too abruptly; just keep him in the path and slow him gradually. Even a tentative kick or two by him should not be reprimanded by a yank on the reins yet. Your main job right now is to communicate to him that what you want is for him to keep going on the path while you are walking behind him. However, if he persists in kicking, you have a problem that must be solved as soon as you have him convinced of what you want. Usually a shaking of the colt's head by sharp, quick, alternate pulls on the line *as* he kicks and a slap of the lines on the stifles will convince him of the error of his ways. However, there is the rare case of the congenital kicker. He must feel the whip and the reprimand of the lines. This takes skill and exact timing, for the punishment must be administered *as* the crime is being committed.

The first lesson on the longlines should be ended as soon as the colt walks a few times each way in the ring. Next day, it may be prolonged, and so on until the colt works calmly and willingly either way of the ring and starts and stops by voice signal. When this stage has been reached, he is ready to be taught to work on the lunge line.

Before returning to a consideration of the lunge line, it may be profitable to digress here and point out that the longlines are very useful in many ways. I have used them on a four-year-old, a good animal with naturally good but high-strung disposition, spoiled by an inept horseman until the animal was considered incorrigible. I first drove him with the longlines with one forefoot tied up with a Rarey strap (pastern fastened to arm close to body). After he had hopped along for some time this way, I put a trip rope on him (rope attached to the ankle strap, then through a ring on the center of the belly band, thence to my hand). He had been so badly spoiled that although he could be ridden, any move on top of him was a signal for a fight. To avoid spoiling his mouth and making other bad matters worse, I used the longlines and soon taught him to pay attention to me and got the notion into his head that I was not just a tormentor, that I was trying to tell him something, and that he would be more comfortable if he tried to get along with me.

In using longlines on a mature animal such as I have just described, it is best to use a bridle with an overcheck. The check rein can be fastened to the saddle or surcingle. With an English saddle, the stirrup leathers can be shortened and brought together just above the pommel, where the check rein can be tied to them with a stout piece of whang leather, unless some more convenient but equally strong means of securing them is devised.

If a bridle with an overcheck is not readily available, a side check rein can be easily added to an ordinary bridle. A stout strap about fifteen inches long, provided with a ring at either end, is securely fastened at its center to the center of the crownpiece of the bridle (laced with whang leather; leather shoelace will do). The rings should be large enough to allow a sash cord to slide through them freely. When the bridle is on the horse, each ring lies just below and slightly behind the juncture of the brow band and the crownpiece of the bridle. Fasten one end of the sash cord to the left ring of a snaffle bit. Then put it through the left ring of the newly added crown strap, then to the fastening on the saddle or surcingle, then to the right ring on the new crownpiece, and finally to the right snaffle ring, where it is fastened.

Whether the overcheck or side rein is used, it should be just tight enough to keep the horse from putting his head lower than his withers. A too tight check rein causes discomfort, bad balance, and frequently a fight. There are only two excuses for a tight check rein. One is its use on a harness racehorse, where it is often very necessary for balance on the trotter or pacer going at thirty miles per hour. The other is its use on a confirmed kicker. In the hands of a professional, the tight check rein may be an aid in breaking a horse of the vice of kicking.

To return to the transition from longline to lunge line, here is the process when everything works well:

Take the left line out of the ring or stirrup so that it runs free from halter to your hand. Then start the colt around the familiar circle to the left (counterclockwise); as the colt walks, you work gradually toward the center of the ring. Without pulling on the lines, keep just sufficient tension on them so you can keep the right line against the colt's stifle (not sagging down to his hock) as you work away from him toward the center of the ring. Finally, you will be able to walk a small circle near the center of the ring, keeping opposite the colt's head and as far from him as the length of the right line will permit. The right line, now behind his stifles, can be shaken a little if he slows to a stop; and a pull on it will keep him from coming in toward the center of the ring if he tries to do so. A few days of work, both ways of the ring, in this fashion will get the idea to him that he is to stay on the trail while you are near the center of the ring. Then you can dispense with the right line as you work to the left.

It is now that the voice signal for stopping, mentioned above, is vital. If it was not well learned at the point indicated above, a little refresher course might well be indulged in before the right line is discarded. The reason for this is that for the first few lessons on the lunge line, the line should not be pulled to stop the colt. So doing will set up the habit of turning toward the center with each "Whoa." Any slight tendency to do so can usually be stopped by a flip of the line if the colt responds to the voice signal.

A few turns around the ring to the left, and the colt is ready to be stopped and reversed. This should be done the first few times by stopping the colt, then going quickly to his head and turning him around. Then you can start leading him to the right and gradually work away from him until he is working at the end of the line. A flip of the line should keep him from crowding toward the center if he starts to do so.

It is obvious that no whip has been used so far in this method. I have worked young horses in all possible maneuvers on the lunge line without laying hands on a whip. Any good trainer should be able to do so. However, after the colt is walking calmly either way of the ring on the line and starting and stopping on command, a whip or a fish pole for signaling is a convenience.

THE WHIP

Before the trainer takes a whip in his hand when he has an animal on a lunge line, he must have thoroughly fixed in his mind that the whip should *never* be used to inflict pain when an animal is on the line. Any use of a whip for such a purpose (justification for such use is rare indeed and requires the utmost in skill and precise timing if it is to do good rather than harm) must be practiced only when the animal is well enough in hand that his every movement can be precisely controlled. From the first lesson, each time the animal is started on a walk, he should be given the distinct voice signal "Walk." "Get up" or any other word or phrase that does not sound too much like signals given for the trot, the gallop, the reverse, or the stop will do as well; but the same signal must be used each time. By the time the whip is introduced, the youngster will have learned the voice signal to start walking the circle. Now, as the voice signal is given, the whip signal can be given simultaneously. To do so, face the animal and have the whip in the right hand (assuming that the horse is traveling the circle to the left) and lunge line in the left. Start with the whip held pointing low to the ground and directly to your right, that is, as far away from the animal as possible without having the whip behind you. As you give the voice signal to walk, bring the whip toward the horse's heels, keeping it close to the ground. Do not bring it close enough to the heels to frighten or cause a kick. After the first few lessons at this, if the animal is a bit on the sluggish side and does not reveal by movement of an ear or eye that he is aware of the movement of the whip, you may raise a little dust with the whip as you bring it toward him.

After a few days of this, you may start using the whip signal with the voice signal for stopping. For the first few times you try this new stunt, reverse the role of the hands just before you stop your pupil. It is best to do so by passing the whip around behind you; keep it low, of course. As you give the voice signal to stop, bring the whip, pointing just barely above the ground, toward the front of the horse.

The number of days which these lessons of starting and stopping with simultaneous voice and whip signals should continue before going on to the next step varies with individual animals. They certainly should be continued until the animal will obey the whip signal without the voice whenever the trainer so desires. Patience and continued repetition will bring far better results than nervous whipping of the ground and stirring up of dust with the whip. After all, if the lunge line is being used to discipline the young horse and to exercise him (assuming he is raised in confined quarters), what is the rush? Each day the lunge line increases his familiarity with human peculiarities, increases the rapport between horse and human, and—if you are as well bred and intelligent for a human as your horse is for one of his kind—increases his enjoyment of doing your bidding.

It is very early springtime as I write these lines. Just a few hours ago I was working a half Quarter Horse filly on a lunge line on a little circle we have worn smooth behind my desert home at the foot of Mummy Mountain. Suddenly, off to my left in the rabbit brush and creosote bush sounded the rather exotic croak of a roadrunner, a fellow who is not very vocal, but spring is in the air, prompting him to the closest thing to a lyrical outburst he can achieve. The filly stopped short and stood, ears pricked. I could not immediately see the vocal runner of the road because his form and color camouflage him effectively in the desert growth; but by following the pointing of the filly's ears, I soon spotted him. I thanked the filly for her aid in my enjoyment of this brief study in natural history. I'm sure the amenity denoted nothing to her, but probably my tone of voice kept up the rapport between us. Her interest in the bird was even more brief than mine; and as I gave her the voice signal to walk, she stepped out smartly. Another recent interruption of our regular workout was accompanied with a bit of violence. Two cats, with their tails bushed and making frightful noises, one chasing the other, rushed across our little ring right in front of the filly. I'm not sufficiently well grounded in felinology to know whether the mad rush was one of amorous dalliance or warfare, though I suspect the initial cause was something erotic. Whatever it was, it excited the filly. A little bit of instant fear and a good deal of curiosity mingled with an urge to play released a lot of quick energy in her little body. She bounced up into the air, turning half away from her line of progress, then by leaps, rears, and high kicks, started in the direction of the vanished cats. I gave her slack for a moment to get the play out of her heels, but saw hysteria taking command, so I gave a quick, very short pull on the line (followed by instant release). This brought her back to sanity if not complete sobriety. Soon we were again at our humdrum academic business. Not completely humdrum, however, for she gave a few bouncy steps as her version of a parade trot now and then and shook her little head.

These two little incidents were not intruded here merely because they are pleasant to recall. They illustrate an attitude toward the young horse that is a prerequisite for making him into a pleasant mount and for making a horse that will someday work his heart out for his rider in a reining arena. I do not feel that the racehorse needs such an attitude and the kind of treatment it prompts. Probably there are other kinds of horses that do not need it, but in the horse whose value depends on working *with* his rider or upon giving his owner pleasure on a casual ride, they are very important. His training must not be a grim business. It should be one that both he and his trainer enjoy. No lesson must be too long. Better three short workouts a day than one too long.

What I have just said does not mean that I or any other experienced horseman overlooks the fact that *there are times when the horse must be forced* to do something he well understands and refuses to do. Such times are rare indeed with *any* horse handled from colthood by an intelligent person. They are more rare than are those occasions on which the would-be masterful horseman mistakes a bit of caprice that is better tolerated (or even enjoyed by the rider) for a vicious act that calls for force. The spoiled pet that has been laughed *at* rather than *with* is often ruined by the exasperated trainer who uses violence on it when firm patience is really the remedy.

COMING TO THE CENTER OF THE RING

After the walk, stop, and reverse at voice and/or whip command are learned, the youngster can be taught to come into the center of the ring on command. To teach him this, stop him; then, pointing the whip straight behind you, pull him toward you while giving a distinct voice signal; "Come here" is as good as any. Of course, always use the same signal. When the youngster comes to you, give him a bit of carrot or apple (I refrain from saying sugar to avoid offending or arousing the ire of many good friends and professionals, should they hear these lines repeated). For the first few times, it is best to lead the horse back to the outside of the circle before resuming work. Later the whip can be pressed against his shoulder or the side of his neck to turn him toward it. Do not be in a hurry to make him return to the outside of the ring without your walking by his shoulder. Take many days, using the pressure of the whip very gradually and increasing it slightly each day.

After this lesson is learned, you may have to use the whip some to keep the pupil from crowding toward the inside of the ring. To do so, pointing the whip at his shoulder may be sufficient. Care must be taken to prevent his confusing this with the bringing of the whip in toward his front, which is a signal to stop. You may even have to pass the whip behind you before you point at his shoulder. If a mere pointing of the whip does not keep him from crowding in toward the center, pat the ground to stir up a little dust and discontinue the carrot of reward for coming to the center. (With some animals this had best be discontinued after the first day or two. Some animals, like some people, seem incapable of getting their minds on anything else when food is in prospect.)

THE TROT

The next logical step in lunge-line work is teaching the trot, a very simple matter. Simply increase the horse's speed by a little stirring of the whip on the ground toward his rear. If he breaks into a gallop, you have probably stirred too much. If he does not drop back into a trot of his own volition, bring the whip in toward his shoulder while repeating the voice signal, "Trot," which, of course, was given as you started him. The work on the trot, both ways of the ring, should be continued until he works perfectly on command. Many horsemen feel that each gait should be taken from a standstill. I see no harm in taking the trot and the gallop from a walk (but never the gallop from the trot). When the trot lesson is well learned, the colt is ready to learn to gallop. I say "gallop" because I prefer to retain the use of the word "canter" for a gait that cannot be taught on the lunge line. Of course, the word "canter" is today often applied to a sloweddown gallop, but to me, the horse that canters brings his jaw in on a light rein, pulls his hocks under him, and rocks along with much of his weight on his haunches.

Probably more skill is needed in teaching the gallop than any other gait performed on the lunge line. Good work on the gallop will have a great influence on the kind of balance the horse will have later and will certainly do much toward giving him dexterity in changing leads, to say nothing of the even more important skill of holding the proper lead. (We fuss so much today about changing leads that we are getting horses that cannot go out and gallop squarely and hold a lead.) The horse can learn on the lunge line to "follow his nose," to avoid "rubbernecking," to have body flexion, and many other useful things, some of which may seem occult at the moment; but I shall try to make them clear and simple as we proceed.

THE GALLOP

Work on the lunge line should be done with only enough tension on the line to keep it off the ground. Many good trainers use a slight, quick flip of the line in conjunction with the voice and/or whip signal for starting, stopping, reverse, and any other change of movement. Some use a series of small flips on the line to help keep the horse from crowding toward the center. However, this flipping technique can be overdone, for one of the important benefits of the lunge line is the opportunity it affords for teaching the horse to work on any gait without tossing his head, and the injudicious use of the line as a signal for a change of movement may promote head tossing. Another cause of head tossing, especially at the gallop, is the practice of using the heavy cavalry or English-type cavesson with the lunge line attached to the nose ring instead of to the ring under the jaw, where I prefer to use it.

I prefer to start the gallop from a walk. The way to do so is, of course, similar to the way in which the horse was first asked to trot. Give him the voice signal "Gallop" and stir the ground behind him with the whip sufficiently to give him the impulsion needed. At this first gallop, especially, he should have a slack line, for any pull on the line is likely to make him twist slightly in his line of progress and lead off with the outside foot in front, resulting in a disunited gallop or a false lead. Of course, whatever he starts on at this first gallop should be allowed to continue for a few strides, for if he is checked (told to stop) immediately, he will assume that he has erred in attempting to gallop. After he has taken a few strides, if he is on the wrong lead, he should be stopped and walked a short distance. Then he should be started again on the gallop. It may take several tries before he hits a good, square gallop on the proper lead. You should be careful not to give him so much impulsion with the whip that he jumps off at a mad dash and gallops too fast. Of course, if your first try results in only a fast trot (which should be stopped after a few strides), you may have to startle him rather smartly with the whip on the ground to get him to break. Then he will start off on a gallop with too much speed. Control this gradually by bringing the whip around behind you and then in front of the horse.

THE LEADS

If you are not sufficiently experienced to recognize leads instantly, it is important to correct your ignorance before you start working an animal at the gallop on the lunge line. The best way to do so is to get a professional or other experienced horseman on a well-schooled horse to demonstrate. Before doing so—for the lesson may be expensive and certainly, if successful, it will be time consuming—here is what to look for:

The properly trained horse leads with the inside forefoot on any turn (unless as a stunt he is asked to maintain a false lead). When a horse is galloping or cantering around you in a circle to the left, he starts by raising his left forefoot. As he does so, his right hind foot strikes the ground and carries his weight. The impact of the right hind is followed by the simultaneous impact of the left hind and right fore (these two diagonal ones working together). Then comes the impact of the leading foot (the left forefoot). Obviously, the leading foot has remained off the ground during the succession of impacts of the other three feet (two of them making impact simultaneously). This means that it rose higher off the ground than did any other foot. This high rise of the leading foot is the first thing you will be able to recognize in learning about leads. When the horse circles about to the right, the succession of impacts with the ground will be (1) left hind, (2) right hind and left fore simultaneously, and (3) right fore.

The disunited gallop or canter, sometimes called crossfiring, is said to be one lead in front and the other behind. For example, if the horse is going to the left on a circle, the succession of hoof impacts is (1) left hind, (2) right hind and right fore simultaneously, and (3) left fore. This disunited canter is quickly recognized when you are riding the horse, for it is very uncomfortable. It is also dangerous on rough ground or wherever a horse might stumble and fall.

PROGRESS AT THE GALLOP

Although many professional trainers feel that on the lunge line the trot is the gait that is most beneficial, I would not rate it above the gallop. Of course, the horse that has learned to hold his trot (never breaks into a gallop unless signaled to do so) and has learned to figure-eight at the trot has benefited greatly. His muscles are developed and he has learned to "follow his nose," an important part of balance in anything he will later be asked; that is, in making turns such as those of the figure eight, his nose always points in the direction of the turn, and his body flexes almost imperceptibly (in contrast to the rigid body and neck of the horse trained on a dumb jockey and also in contrast to the horse that has to be pulled into a turn with his head yawing off toward the inside of the turn).

Perfecting the gallop on the lunge line takes much time and patience. While doing so, the walk and the trot should not be neglected. After the youngster has learned to take the proper (inside) lead immediately on signal, going either way of the ring, he is ready to be taught to change leads while galloping. To do so, he must do a figure eight and change leads as he reaches the outside of the ring, going in a new direction. To teach this skill, start the youngster to the left on the left lead. After he makes a round or two, bring him across the center of the ring and head him into the trail he has just left, but going to the right. Just as his nose is at the circle, heading toward the right, a quick impulsion from the whip—a flick of the lash in the air or a tap on the ground, or whatever is needed for the particular temperament of the horse—should be given. If your timing is right and your knowledge of your pupil has enabled you to give the proper amount of impulsion, you will get an instant change of lead. If there is no change, stop the horse, reverse him, and try again, this time using a little more impulsion *just as* he noses into the reverse trail. If you get a change only in front, resulting in a disunited gallop, you *may* complete the change and get a true lead by inducing a quick burst of speed. However, if the colt you are working is highly excitable, this may be a poor method, and you had better stop him and try again. Perfecting this flying change of leads will most certainly take many days, probably weeks, and possibly months. No one lesson at the gallop should be long or in the least tiring. Long workouts for developing muscles when the animal is big enough to be mounted should be done largely at the trot.

SADDLING AND BRIDLING

The young horse that has been sensibly and regularly worked on a lunge line since he was a foal presents no problem in saddling and bridling when he is mature enough to be ridden. The age at which he reaches this stage varies with the individual horse, and the way in which he has been fed and the manner in which he will be ridden. Many potential winners on the track are crippled by being ridden as long yearlings or two-year-olds. However, it does no harm to a two-year-old, if he has been properly fed and is in good condition, to put a light rider on him for a few minutes at a time. Contrary to public opinion, it is not the back that will first show signs of damage by too much riding at too early an age (unless, of course, the animal has a conformational back defect); it is the legs and the feet. If the owner is inexperienced, he will do well to consult his veterinarian about the fitness of his colt for work.

If the two-year-old is ready for very light work under saddle and has never been saddled, the place to start is in his stall, with the colt tied or held by an assistant. The saddle to use is the lightest, simplest saddle available; for example, an English saddle from which the stirrups are readily removable—and replaceable. A racing saddle is, of course, lighter but cannot be ridden with any comfort or security to the rider. If you have a colt to saddle and have access only to a Western saddle, tie the stirrups securely across the seat of the saddle. Tie all saddle strings securely across the skirt in the rear and to the horn in front. Remove the hind cinch if the saddle is fully rigged and tie the rear cinch billets securely to the saddle strings so that there will be nothing flapping around the colt's flanks the first time he wears it.

If the lining of the saddle is in good condition, no blanket need be used the first time the colt is saddled. If a blanket is needed, it should be presented to the colt, like the saddle, so that he can smell it and put his lips on it if he so desires. Take care to see that he does not pull it from your hands so it will flop and frighten him. After carefully laying the blanket on the colt's back, keep a hand on it, so that a sudden move on his part does not make it fall and frighten him. A quick, quiet, and intelligent assistant is very useful at this time; however, none at all is better than one that giggles and is afraid of getting close to the animal. All this early work with saddling should be done with your body close to the colt. Many a young animal has been frightened by the timid handler who pokes equipment at him with outstretched arms.

Place the saddle quietly and firmly on the back. Gradually cinch or girth it just tight enough to prevent it from falling off. Untie the colt and lead him about the stall. If he seems a bit nervous about the saddle, lead him about until he is at ease. Then tie him up again and unsaddle him.

At the second lesson he can, after being led about his stall until he is at ease with the saddle, be led out of it, walked for a few minutes, and returned to his stall. If this lesson goes well, you may, at the next lesson, lean your weight across the saddle, then put a little weight on one side of it.

When walking about with a saddle on his back and having you put a little weight on it now and then is a totally acceptable business for the colt, let down the stirrups. Do this first in the stall with the colt tied or held by an assistant, so that you can let them down carefully; and after the colt is well aware of their presence, stroke him and move the stirrups about some, so that he will see that they are harmless. Then untie him, lead him about the stall, and finally outside.

FIRST MOUNTING

The first mounting should be done in the stall; however, if the roof is too low for the comfort of the rider, it will have to be done in the corral. Pick a place where the colt will be inclined to stay put; for instance, a corner where he can be tied or held facing the fence. The first lesson should consist only of slipping quietly onto his back, sitting there only long enough for him to become quiet and nibble at a bit of feed. The next day will be soon enough to let him walk about the stall or corral. When you do so, let *him* start the walk. If a good assistant is at hand to lead him, so much the better.

The first objective of this stage of training is to communicate to the colt that it is perfectly harmless for him to walk around in the stall or corral with someone on his back. It is usually easier to communicate this to a colt by having an assistant to lead him than it is to allow him to start of his own volition. Without the aid of an assistant, plenty of time has to be given the colt to allow him to take the first tentative step. With all colts except those that have a peculiar disposition and those with whom the trainer has not established the right kind of relationship, that first step with a rider on his back will not be a violent or fast one. However, if he does start out too fast, he can almost invariably be slowed down and calmed by being turned in a very short circle.

To turn a colt in such a circle, grasp the rein on the side toward the center of the stall or corral as close to the bit as you conveniently can. Then pull out to the side as far as possible and do not raise your hand above the level of the colt's back. If you do this properly, he will turn in a small circle like a cat chasing its tail. He will not continue long to pursue his tail; and just as soon as he calms down, you will release the pull.

The same kind of pull is useful in teaching the colt to start on signal. During these first few mounted lessons, never use your feet or legs to start the colt moving. To start him to move, use the kind of pull I have just described. However, you will use that pull just long enough to get him to move one foot. As soon as he moves that one foot, release the pull and pet the colt. Usually after he takes that first step, he will continue walking. However, if he takes the one step and stops, repeat the performance. Your second pull does not necessarily have to be on the same side as the first one. Soon the colt will get the idea that a pull to the side means to start walking.

Just as soon as the colt loses his fear of moving with weight on his back, you should take care to mount him only when his head is in a corner of the corral or at least facing directly into the fence of the corral. If you have an assistant, he can aid you by standing at the colt's head in such a way as to discourage any tendency to move forward as you are mounting.

One of the first and most important things for a horse to learn when he is old enough to be mounted is that he must stand still while being mounted and remain stationary until told to move. It is easy to establish the habit of standing for mounting if all temptation to move is removed during the early mounting lessons; it is difficult and irritating to break the habit of moving out or twisting about the moment a rider's foot is in the stirrup.

The descriptions of horses found in Western fiction by writers whose lives have been spent east of the Great Lakes often depict them taking off in a cloud of dust the moment a boot touches a stirrup. This may make colorful fiction, but today's buyers and show-ring standards dictate that the horse that will not stand until told to move is a very inferior creature.

MOUNTING THE HORSE UNGENTLED BY LUNGE LINE

It is possible to mount without a fight the horse that has never had previous work on the lunge line, or otherwise, to gentle him. The steps I have just outlined are the ones to take, but they must be taken more slowly than with the young horse that has learned that his trainer is to be trusted and that a human's moves have meaning. (To some horses, any human move is a sign of impending pain!)

A somewhat tragic first mounting of a green horse, which occurred near my home just a few days ago, may emphasize some of the things necessary to know when handling the very green horse.

A neighbor has a five-year-old gelding which he raised in a corral at his suburban home. The gelding was broken to lead and to stand tied. He seemed well disposed but had never been worked with on a lunge line, longlines, or any other way. Another neighbor, a well-intentioned young man, volunteered to ride the gelding.

On the appointed afternoon, onlookers assembled to watch the performance; that was the first mistake. (When a green colt is learning, he should not be distracted or frightened by onlookers.) The horse was tied to the corral fence, a bit nervous because of the audience. The young man brought out the saddle and did let the horse smell it; but before the animal had satisfied its curiosity, the saddle was slipped on its back and cinched up just a bit tighter than necessary. The young horse trembled slightly but stood rigid. Then, using wise precaution, the young man slipped the headstall of a bridle up under the nose band of the halter and over the gelding's ears, forcing the bit into its mouth. Then the halter was unbuckled and slid off the head. The horse, still rigid, stood while the young man gave it a few strokes on the neck with the flat of his hand.

At this point the onlookers became vocal with, "Ride him, Harry!" "Coming out of chute number five!" and other equally intelligent remarks.

The young man mounted. The corral-raised gelding, unlike his predecessors of the days of the open range, who would have bogged ahead and tossed the young man twenty feet, stood and broke into a profuse sweat.

At this point, if the onlookers could have been made to vanish quietly into thin air and the young man had sat quietly for some fifteen or twenty minutes—maybe even less—that gelding would probably have relaxed. In a bit longer time, he would undoubtedly have moved a foot, and eventually moved another, and so on until he was walking about the corral quietly. The rider could then have started giving him a little direction if the bit had been suitable—a snaffle, not the curb which was in the horse's mouth. However, the onlookers, instead of vanishing, became more vocal. The rider became a bit nervous, tugged at one rein, then another; kicked with his feet; and clucked with his mouth. He asked someone to bring him a whip, but fortunately, at that moment the young man's father appeared, successfully insisted that the rider dismount, rubbed the now dripping horse down, and tried him another day without an audience.

Frequently, among certain strains of horses raised behind fences, an animal occurs that can go without much handling until it is old enough to ride, and then be ridden by a careful and intelligent horseman without any fight. Such an animal soon learns what a bit means and rapidly becomes a serviceable mount. *No son todos los mismos* (They are not all the same), as a wise old Mexican horseman told me. If my neighbor's five-year-old gelding had been handled with more care and patience, he would, in a very few lessons, have learned what was wanted of him and would have done so without fear, sweat, or fight.

His first saddling should have been done without an audience. He should have been allowed plenty of time to inspect the saddle and the blanket. If the young man had had no opportunity to let the gelding wear a bit in the stall or corral for a few minutes each day for several days prior to the first mounting the bit should have been put into his mouth as gently as possible; and then he should have been allowed to stand or been led about the stall or corral for a few minutes while he mouthed it and got the feel of the saddle. Then he should have been returned to the stall or a corner of the corral where he could not readily move forward immediately when mounted.

When such a horse stands still upon first being mounted, he should be given time to do so as long as he wishes. (This is, of course, not to be confused with the action of the spoiled horse or the one raised on the open range who knows man only as the creature who ropes him, brands him, castrates him, and never comes near him except to do something painful or frightening. Such a horse may freeze for a moment upon first being mounted, but the freeze is just the calm before the storm. He comes out of the freeze with an explosion.) Even if such a horse as my neighbor's gelding chooses to stand for an hour—I have never seen one do so for more than a few minutes—the hour will be well spent just sitting on him and letting him find out that no harm is intended by his rider. The horse should be the one to make the first move. The reins should be used only enough to steady him to a walk should he start at a faster gait.

In those rare instances when a young horse under his first saddle starts to run and become hysterical, he should be checked by what some horsemen call "bending." This is simply turning the horse in a short circle by a strong lateral pull. The pull is given on a short rein, with the hand held low and well out to the side. It is doubtful that my neighbor's gelding would have stampeded if he had been allowed to stand until he was ready to move; but had he done so, bending would have immediately steadied him. Then he could have been allowed to walk about the corral or open field with as little direction from his rider as possible until the animal had relaxed.

In spite of mishandling, my neighbor's gelding, because of his unusually good disposition, is showing signs of becoming a serviceable mount, though I suspect he will always be a head tosser and a bit on the spooky side.

FIRST BITS

Were I responsible for the choice of the proper bit for the first riding of a specific animal, I'd be more concerned about the hand on the reins than about the kind of horse wearing the bit. While my own choice is a bosal and a bit hung unused in the mouth for early riding, there are very, very few professional trainers I would permit to use such equipment on a colt of mine. (There are two or three old-timers on ranches I know whom I'd be happy to have use it.) Probably the bit that will fit most hands today is the snaffle. The eggbutt is probably the best type of snaffle for the green horse, though the big-ringed Irish bridoon is about as good. Leather guards around the mouthpiece just outside the corners of the mouth on any other kind of snaffle are imperative to keep from making the corners of the mouth sore; and they do no harm on the eggbutt or the Irish bridoon either.

The number of bits, manufactured and homemade, for use on the green horse would fill a catalog. I recently saw, on a very respectable breeding farm, a Springsteen bit on a filly being ridden for the third saddle. The Springsteen has iron thumbs that press against the outside of the jaw very painfully. On the same farm I saw, on a green colt, a specially made bit, a sort of curb equipped with little pulleys and a stout cord. It was so made that when the reins (which were attached to the ends of the cord) were pulled, the cord pressed across the soft part of the nose as the curb pressed upon the bars of the mouth. I also saw being used, on green youngsters, two different kinds of hackamore bits. It is possible that each one of these pieces of equipment was advantageously used. *No son todos los mismos.* Peculiar horses sometimes respond best to peculiar bits, but the safest policy for most horsemen is to let the other fellow experiment, especially with bits that may cause much pain. Many a horse that might have had a delightful mouth is made into a confirmed head tosser, bit fighter, or puller by the use of a trick bit of some sort when he is first ridden.

A good snaffle equipped with a chinstrap running from bit ring to bit ring under the jaw, just tight enough to afford some pressure when a strong lateral pull is exerted on one rein, is the best bit for most modern hands on most green horses. For any hand that can manage two sets of reins, the ideal equipment is one pair of reins attached to the snaffle and running free and another pair running through a martingale. A colt's immediate reaction to any kind of restraint is like that of a child—resistance. The first pull on a snaffle bit is almost always met by a forward thrust of the nose. This, of course, makes the snaffle pull toward the ears on the corners of the mouth. If the rider has sufficiently long arms, he may be able to get his hands low enough to get the pull downward on the bars, but a running martingale with the rings adjusted so they will come no higher than a few inches below the withers is a sure means of getting the pull where it belongs.

When using two sets of reins, take the pair on one side in your hand with knuckles (back of hand) toward the horse's ears and finger pointing across the horse's withers. The free rein should come into your hand by passing over the base of the index finger. Then it falls downward across the palm, leaving the hand at the base of the little finger. The rein running through the martingale comes into the hand at the base of the little finger and passes upward across the palm and out of the hand at the base of the forefinger. This means that the reins cross each other in the palm of the hand, where they are gripped by the fingers. The thumb clamps down on the two reins at the base of the forefinger. When the reins are so held, a slight twist of the wrist will enable you to exert pressure on either rein alone or on the two of them equally. The free rein is the one to use except at such times as the colt thrusts his nose out or up.

EARLY RIDING IN OPEN COUNTRY

Opinions differ on the advisability of riding a young horse in the open country when he is in training. Many winning show horses of all types have never been ridden outside an arena. My firm conviction is that they would have been even better show horses had they been given plenty of quiet riding in the open and also been let out on a good free gallop now and then when they were being taught their early lessons. It is wise to ride the colt the first few times in a small corral, where he can get over any fear he may have of being ridden and learn to trot and gallop without panic. Certainly the corral is extremely useful in teaching the colt to rein, stop, change or hold leads, and so on; but no horse ridden only in an arena is useful outside the arena, and many an arena horse would profit from a little work in the open.

As soon as the colt has lost all fear of being ridden at any gait in the corral or arena, he is ready to go outside. When you first take one out, a companion mounted on a good steady horse is a big help. The old horse will give the youngster confidence. However, it is better to be alone than with a companion mounted on a silly or sluggish horse.

On the first trip, don't ask the colt to turn or stop just for the sake of turning or stopping. Don't ask him for much of anything on that first ride. Enjoy the scenery and hope the colt does the same. Just see to it that he does not rush. If he walks all the time on that first ride, fine. A little jog now and then will do no harm. If he stops and wants to stare now and then, also fine. I have no patience with the martinet who demands constant alert attention to the rider at all times. Such a one rarely has a willing worker under his saddle. Half the fun of riding is enjoying it *with* the horse. I have seen deer, elk, wild turkeys, and even a lion or two, to say nothing of the countless small interesting things, both animate and inanimate, that I would have missed without the keen ears of my mount to point them out to me. The relation a horse is to have with his rider is largely determined during his first riding. Long experience has taught me that the horse that enjoys a ride in the open can be more willingly attentive to his rider when work is to be done than can a horse ridden by the demanding martinet.

After your colt has learned that open-country riding is not fraught with hidden perils, you can begin to turn him in and out among a group of trees or other obstacles. Stop him and ask him to stand for a few seconds—not long enough to start a fight but long enough to let him know that standing still is part of the game.

Many a horse has been well started in the vice of shying on his first ride in the open. If yours was raised in a corral, open country is full of things beyond his comprehension. Most humans fear what they cannot understand. Would you demand more bravery from a colt? If your colt wants to give a strange object a wide berth on the first ride out in the open, humor him. There is plenty of time on later rides to dismount, touch the object with your hand, and entice the colt to test it with his nose. (When he does so, be sure to have the reins well in hand so you can go with him if he flies back from it.) There may come a time when a whip or spur has to be used to convince him that your command takes precedence over his fear, but not at this stage of the game. All good teachers know how important it is to know when to ignore minor misbehavior.

These early rides are primarily to teach what a bit is for, what leg pressure means, and that a good colt stops when asked and starts the same way. When he is walking along quietly, leave his head alone. Let him chew that bit on a slack rein. When you want to turn him, keep your hand low and pull well out to the side, using the rein through the martingale only if his head thrusts upward and his nose pokes forward. After a few rides you can begin to use a very light neck-rein pressure well forward on his neck *as* you use the lateral pull. It will be many, many rides before you can use the neck rein alone, but if you are consistent in its use and increase the neck-rein pressure *very* gradually, you will have a well-reined horse that does not fight the rein or twist its head to the side when reined.

In stopping, you will probably have to use the rein through the martingale or hold your hand very low if using a single rein, for most green horses thrust their heads up and forward for some time when pulled to a stop. Until the young horse learns that the pull on the reins is a signal to stop, not just discomfort inflicted at random, do not try any quick stops. The martingale is usually as helpful in starting as in stopping, for unless the colt is quite eager to move forward at every opportunity, he will have to be turned slightly to the side to get him started. Never just sit on a colt and kick him to start forward.

"Rubbernecking," bending the neck without turning the body, is quite common and natural among very green animals, even those that have been taught to follow their noses. Avoid rubber-necking. This fault should not be allowed to continue beyond the first few lessons. To aid in putting a stop to it, the colt must be taught to respond to the leg aids so you can ride "both ends of him." Perhaps the most common fault of amateur riders is that they ride only one end of the horse. That is, they control only the forehand and are utterly helpless when their mounts twist their hindquarters from side to side or insist on going sidewise.

Start teaching the leg aid* from the ground. Standing close to your horse's left shoulder and facing his croup, hold the reins, both or all of them, in your left hand close to his jaw. With your right hand push his hip until he moves his hindquarters one step to the side—away from you. Your left hand keeps his forequarters from moving. Now, stand on the other side, reversing the jobs of your hands, and move the hindquarters a step to the side. One step on each side may be enough for the first lesson, depending on the temperament of the colt. Never continue this first lesson so long that you start a fight. A few hours later or the next day you may give a second lesson. Gradually more than one step may be achieved. When the colt gets the idea and readily moves his quarters at the touch of your hand on his hip while you are keeping his forequarters still, you may gradually, lesson by lesson, shift the position of the pushing hand until it is pushing at the spot where your heel will press when you are mounted. Finally,

---

* The leg aid actually starts as a "foot aid" with all but extremely nervous or responsive horses. After the horse is perfectly trained, a mere
movement of the leg of the rider is all that is needed to get the desired
response, though heel and even spur are occasionally used on the most
refined of horses.

before you attempt to move his quarters when you are mounted, use only the thumb of the pushing hand on the horse's side where your heel will press when mounted. If you prefer, the butt of a whip or a blunt spur may be used instead of your thumb.

The transition from the thumb pressure to the heel pressure when mounted should be gradual. First, get an assistant to stand by the horse's shoulder and hold the reins close to the jaw to steady the forequarters while you, sitting in the saddle, apply heel pressure. If the horse does not immediately respond to the heel, have the assistant use his thumb. If the horse is not too high-strung, you may find that a blunt spur means more to him than the heel of your boot. Gradually the assistant may turn command over to you. However, for some time do not attempt more than a yielding to heel pressure while the forequarters remain stationary. Two or three steps to either side is enough response at this stage.

When such response is prompt and willing, you may start to ask the horse to shift his hindquarters a trifle while walking. Finally, you can get him to two-track a few steps at the walk. This means that he will walk, making tracks with his hind feet that are a little to the side of the tracks made by the forefeet. Eventually you will be able to two-track at the trot. At the gallop, ask a horse to put his quarters only to the side on which he is leading. To do otherwise is to court disaster. If the horse should try to obey you and attempt to carry his hindquarters to the right when he is on the left lead (or vice versa), he may fall or injure a leg.

With the finished horse, the most useful function of the leg aid is that of keeping the hindquarters from twisting to the outside on a turn. So the final and most important lessons (which may well come much later in training) in response to the leg aid should consist of keeping his hindquarters stationary while he turns his forehand to either side. Eventually you should be able to inscribe a circle of about three feet in diameter with a pointed stick in the ground, stop your mount with his hind feet in the circle, and turn his forehand completely around while his hind feet remain in the circle.

Another useful trick for your horse to learn at a much later date is the side pass. In that movement, you move his hindquarters to the side with the leg aid and the forequarters to the same side with the reins. Both ends of the horse move at exactly the same speed, so he moves sidewise in a straight line at a right angle to the direction he faces.

The leg aid alone will not cure the habit of rubbernecking. Of course, it will enable you to keep the horse's body in line with his neck, which is a big help at slow speeds on early lessons. However, when a horse turns at any speed beyond a slow walk, he must not turn on his forequarters. To do so at high speed is likely to cripple him (though there are some horses that can do so without disaster; for example, the bull-fighting Pasos of Peru). If, for instance, a horse turns to the left by twisting his hindquarters to the right, he turns on his forefeet, his forehand. In a correct turn at high speed, the horse balances on his haunches and lifts the forequarters around in the direction of the turn. If he tends to twist his hindquarters toward the outside of the turn, the leg aid is used as a preventive.

The extent to which the leg aid helps to prevent rubbernecking is limited, and that limit is reached as soon as the colt begins to travel under saddle faster than a walk. From that stage on, the reins are the chief factor for some time. The first use of the reins in getting the horse to turn was a pull very low and far out to the side. Gradually that pull can be made less a sidewise one, just a short pull on the side toward which the turn is wanted. This pull is accompanied by pressure of the neck rein, far forward and very slight at first. If the colt tends to rubberneck, change the pull to a series of very short and, if necessary, sharp pulls. There is a current fashion for using a bat on the shoulder on the side opposite the one toward which the horse is turning. A deft hand will not need a bat. A sluggish colt may have to be urged forward by strong use of the heel for a turn. If so, he should first be taught what the heels mean. Teach him by using the heels each time you turn him a little to start him. Do so very gently at first, of course.

After the young horse has learned to stand while being mounted, start, stop, respond to leg aid, pay some attention to neck rein (not necessarily to the point of needing no lateral pull at all), and work quietly in open country, he is ready for faster and more demanding work in the arena or training corral.

7

THE REINING HORSE

To develop the reining horse, never do any training when the horse is tired. A horse that is in excellent physical condition and not overworked will, in the hands of a good trainer, easily develop a light mouth and quick response to the rein. A horse that is not quite in the pink will rarely do so.

Horses, like children, vary in natural ability. Not all humans can learn to sing opera, fight in the ring, or design buildings. Great stars in any field are not born daily. So it is with horses. The great reining horse or cutting horse is one among thousands of foals.

The attempt to make a top reining horse out of a colt that is naturally endowed only to win races or the attempt to train the undernourished or overworked will probably lead to the use of shortcuts and gimmicks and will be as useless—or harmful—as the attempt to make a finished horse in a hurry. Some of the commonly used gimmicks are painful tiedowns (chains over the head, wire or cable nose bands), the use of tacks in boot toes or bats, and sawed off icepicks to jab the neck and shoulders. There are now on the market and advertised occasionally in horse magazines, devices that deliver an electric shock through the reins to the side of the neck. Such gimmicks, if the horse and rider survive their use, may produce a horse that will sell to the unwary, but will not make a horse that I would like to ride, and I doubt that any horse trained with such devices will put out the performance needed in better show-ring competition.

When the young horse is ready for intense and specialized training for reining, he needs a competent trainer and lots of time. He must develop a mouth so light that his forequarters can be lifted off the ground for a quarter-turn to right or left by a slight raising of the hand with light pressure on the reins. To develop such a mouth, never lug on the reins; if your horse does not respond to a pull, repeat it in rapid succession with increasing sharpness and quickness until you get results. If you ask for a left turn and he does not respond or turns his nose to the right as you lay the right rein on his neck to signal a left turn, a quick, sharp pull out to the side on the left rein may solve the problem.

Assuming, of course, that the horse is sufficiently advanced in preliminary training to be ready for work in fast reining—that he knows what the rein means—insist on obedience to a given signal until you get it, but don't rub it in. Don't repeat it until the horse sours completely on the movement. Once you gain your point, let that movement rest until tomorrow.

THE LOW HEAD

Western horses in horse shows are a relatively new phenomenon. Before their advent, a show horse's most obvious feature was his high head carriage. It took years for the Western newcomers to realize that the high head carriage was not their cup of tea, and it took more years for them to realize that the low head carriage is a virtue in certain situations. When they did come to the realization, they made a fetish of the low head. My veterinarian, who is well acquainted with local training establishments, recently remarked that a thirty-inch piece of iron pipe with one end taped as a handle is standard equipment in training stables. The pipe is used, of course, to hit the horse over the head to make him keep it down. When I asked how the trainers avoid fistula of the poll, he said, "Oh, they're smart; they hit the big muscles just behind the poll."

This practice is certainly not common among the top trainers in the West, but it indicates something very important in training—avoidance of the high head. Jerking on the reins and striving for fast results are the two chief causes of high heads. The owner who insists on seeing marked results after a trainer has worked with a horse for ninety days is the cause of the use of head beating. The good stock horse works with his head fairly low, that is, the spine of his neck is approximately at right angles to the slope of his shoulders and his neck is flexed just behind the poll. When he is working cattle, especially calves, it will be even lower. He does not need to be beaten over the head or tied down with chains to do so. What he does need is to learn what is wanted without being jerked, yanked, or prodded. Then if he is made of the right stuff, is in good physical condition, and not overworked, he will put his head down naturally where it belongs when he works. I suspect that the trainer who tries to fake the genuine article by the use of gimmicks will receive his due if he gets into real competition with top trainers.

TRAINING FOR REINING

The foundation for any performance is a good walk, trot, and gallop on the straightaway. Without this foundation it is useless to hope for perfection in training of any kind. Your horse must walk up promptly and freely from a standstill at a slight pressure of your legs or shift of pressure on the reins. He must do a good smart walk without showing a tendency to jiggle or jog unless told to do so. He must trot freely from a walk or standstill when asked, and maintain the speed his rider demands. He must do so on a slack rein and without any tendency to rush ahead or to die down. He must gallop freely from a standstill, walk, or trot as his rider requests. He must take whichever lead is asked of him. He must hold his lead on a gallop on a straightaway without any tendency to flop back and forth from one lead to another or become disunited. After starting work on rollbacks, pivots, or other movements that call for changes of leads, it is quite necessary with better horses to do a good deal of work at the gallop on the straightaway so that the horse will maintain a lead and not flop back and forth when there is no call for change.

BITTING THE REINING HORSE

Many a top reining horse will work with any kind of a bit, or halter, or even a clothesline looped around his nose or neck if he is mounted by a competent rider. In many of our shows we have hackamore classes for reining horses. These are carryovers from the days when most trainers used the hackamore rather than the snaffle bit to start a colt on. It is easy to start an argument among experienced horsemen about the best bit to use for a reining horse. Such agreement as there is points to the use of the mild curb bit. The transition from the training snaffle to the curb bit to be used for the reining horse should be a gradual one. The four-ring pelham is an excellent device for accomplishing this transition. Though some good horsemen prefer the jointed four-ring pelham, I prefer the solid one because of the difficulty of adjusting the chain or chinstrap on the jointed pelham so that it will not pinch the corners of the horse's mouth.

The chief advantage of the four-ring pelham in the transition from snaffle to curb is that it permits the use of two pairs of reins. The pair attached to the lower rings of the pelham operates with the leverage action of ordinary curb bits. The pair attached to the upper rings operates without a leverage action and with an effect very similar to that of the snaffle bit. At first, of course, the upper reins alone should be used. Then, after the colt has become thoroughly accustomed to the use of the new bit and the upper reins, the lower reins can begin to come into use. Very gradually increase the use of the lower reins and decrease the use of the upper reins. Ask the colt for only the simplest of movements when first using the new bit. Even after you have started to work him on the lower reins alone, be sure to revert quickly to the use of the upper reins if, by some mischance, you find it necessary to exert any considerable pressure on the reins. This is to prevent developing any fear of the curb in the young horse. It is very important at this stage to remember that the horse's head follows your hand. The high hand means the high head, and the low hand means the low head.

Gradually the young horse will begin to learn what the new bit means. He will eventually be able to perform on the curb bit all those things that he learned to do on the snaffle. When he reaches this stage he will be ready for you to teach him the fast stop.

TEACHING THE STOP

Commence the teaching of the stop at the walk. When your horse has learned to stop the moment you take the slack out of the reins, you should begin to use the leg signal simultaneously with your hand for stopping. This means simply that you give a light squeeze with your legs in front of the cinch just as you take the slack out of the reins with your hands. This may not seem important at the walk, but when you reach the stage of teaching the fast stop from the gallop, it will be very necessary for you to give the horse this slight warning before you release your hand, so that you will not spoil his light mouth by having to tug on the reins. Stopping should not be done repeatedly in the same spot, for this would cause your horse to anticipate. He should learn to stop instantly on signal and should also learn to refrain from stopping unless you signal. At the walk he should learn to stop squarely, that is, without twisting from side to side. If you antici-pate using him for a rope horse, it is advisable to teach him to back a few steps when he stops.

Teaching a horse to stop from a gallop, you should start with the slow lope. As you increase the speed with which you stop at the gallop, the warning you give with your legs should be accom-panied by a warning with the bridle hand. As your horse's fore-

The perfect stop, Monte Foreman up. Note position of horse's head and his closed, relaxed mouth, indicating a light hand on the reins. Note also the absence of tiedown, and the position of rider and his use of leg aid. *Photo courtesy Monte Foreman*

quarters come up in the natural rhythm of the gallop, lift those forequarters lightly with your bridle hand on the stride before the one on which you stop him. At the fast gallop, you should lift him twice before the final stopping. You signal, "Lift, lift, ho."

If all your training up to this point has been good, your horse's hind legs will come up under his weight at the first lift, and at the full signal he will slide those hind feet and put his number eleven down on the ground in the proper fashion. He will stop squarely and will stop without thrusting his nose forward or throwing up his head.

When your horse is doing this fast stop, your weight must be forward in the saddle. If you sit in the rear of your saddle and put your weight on the cantle, your weight will be far behind those hind feet, and you will cause your horse's fetlocks to slide on the ground and be badly skinned. It is a good idea to use boots on the horse's hind ankles (called variously "roping boots," "ankle boots," "skid boots"; procurable at any saddlery store in the West and at most feed stores) at all times when training him to do the fast stop, for a bit of uneven ground may cause him to bruise a fetlock even if your weight is where it belongs and you are stopping properly. To bruise a hind fetlock will most certainly make the horse dislike the stop.

TIEDOWNS

Most ropers, especially those who earn all or part of their living by roping, use standing martingales (tiedowns). Their attention is on the calf. They can't be bothered about giving the horse a warning for the stop. His warning is the throwing of the rope, and the pressure of the rider's left hand on the horse's neck is the final signal. Any yank on the mouth to stop may be rather hard, because the rider is tense and certainly in a big hurry. A few ropers are prone to give a yank on the reins even when it is unnecessary. The only way for such riders to keep a horse's head down is to tie it down. Of course, not all well-trained horses survive such treatment, but there seem to be enough of them that do to keep a number of such ropers mounted.

Whether you are training your horse to use for your own enjoyment or to use in reining competition, the chances are very good that you will do well to avoid the use of the tiedown in training. As I have previously stated, the head follows the hand, and the horse that learns to stop without a tiedown, keeping his head where it belongs, is a better trained animal than one that requires a tiedown. It is always possible to put a standing martingale (tiedown) on a well-trained horse that will work well without it, but it is impossible to do fast work on a horse trained with a tiedown unless the tiedown is put on him.

BACKING

The best time to teach a horse to back is when he is a tiny foal. If he has not been taught to back at the voice signal and to back willingly and straight, it is best to wait until he is thoroughly accustomed to the leg aid. The leg aid I refer to here is the pressure of the calf of your leg against the horse's ribs behind the cinch. In response to this pressure, he should readily move his hindquarters away from the side on which the pressure is applied.

The first teaching of the mature horse to back should be done from the ground. Until your horse will back readily at voice signal, give all the lessons at the same spot. This should be beside a fence or a building. When the horse's right side, let us say, is close to a fence or building, he cannot swing his quarters to the right. This cuts in half your problem of keeping him backing in a straight line.

Stand directly in front of your horse, close to him. In your left hand grasp close to his jaw the reins of a snaffle bit or the reins attached to the top rings of a four-ring pelham. Say "Back" and press on his nose with your right hand and pull back and slightly downward on the reins with your left hand. With nine horses out of ten, if the proper relationship exists between horse and trainer, the horse will respond by taking a backward step. If your horse does not so respond, lead him away from the fence, walk him in a small circle, bring him back to the fence again, and start all over. This time when you stand in front of him, stand about three feet in front of his head. As you press on his nose, put pressure on the reins and say "Back," step forward one step quickly toward his head, bringing your chest in contact with his nose if possible. If he takes the one backward step, relax and praise him.

There are, of course, the rare horses who seem to have a congenital aversion to backing. Probably the truth about such horses is that some experience in their growing up has made them afraid of backing or has aroused their anger at the idea. Whatever the cause, such horses present a problem. If you have one of them, your chief concern should be to discover a way to get the horse to take a backward step without fighting him or causing him pain. To cause pain at this point is merely to add fuel to the flame. I have solved some such problems by leading the horse to a gate with his head as close to it as possible. Then, as a helper opened the gate against the horse, forcing him backward, I said "Back"; this is a stunt worth trying on any difficult horse. Of course, a barn door, if it opens outward, will do as well as a gate. The first backward step may not be too straight, but don't be too fussy about that first step, and don't repeat it immediately. If you achieve that first backward step, praise the horse (and your Maker). Then lead him about or do anything else casual with him to get his mind off backing before you try to get him to take another backward step. Much patience at this stage is far better than the use of force or pain.

I have seen draw reins, tack collars, bats, and electric prods used on horses that objected to taking a backward step. In each instance, the trainer had a long, hard row to hoe. If you must resort to force, here is one more trick that is worth trying: Have your horse close to a fence. Then let a helper put one end of a stout ten- or twelve-foot pole a few inches through the fence about the height of the horse's shoulder or a few inches higher, so that when the pole is held by your helper at right angles to the fence it will press on your horse's chest or on the lower part of the front of his neck. With your helper on the end of the pole, using it as a lever to press backward on your horse's chest or neck, you will tell the horse "Back" and press backward on his nose and on the reins. This stunt must be done quietly, of course, without yelling or jumping about.

In the first few lessons in backing, any backward step is success. If your horse takes one or more backward steps, whether in a straight line or not, let him know he has done well. Gradually you can increase the number of backward steps to three or four. Then you can begin to give attention to the straightness of the backing. If the right side of your horse is against the fence or wall, you have only to pay attention to the left side to be sure that it does not swing out away from the fence. Do not be too exacting at first, but gradually, with your hand against the horse's ribs behind the cinch, you can keep his quarters in line. Continue these lessons from the ground until your horse will back readily in a straight line for eight or ten steps. Then you are ready to try backing when you are mounted.

The first few lessons in backing the mounted horse should be given in the same spot where the lessons in backing from the ground were given. This will mean, of course, that your left leg against the horse's ribs behind the cinch will keep him from swinging his quarters away from the fence when he backs. These first few mounted lessons in backing will be given when your horse is quietly standing still.

The next step is to walk him briskly to the spot where you have been teaching him to back. Stop him and immediately back him a few steps. When he will do this readily, he is ready to be trotted up to the spot and backed. When this has been accomplished, he is ready to be galloped up to the same spot and backed a few steps in a straight line. When he will do this readily, he is ready to be any place in the arena away from the fence, stopped, and backed.

Never precipitate a fight with a horse when it is possible to avoid one. When your horse has one of his "bad days" or is in a particularly unresponsive mood, you can tell in the first few trips you take around the ring to warm him up that any demand for precise or fast work will probably bring on a fight. On such a day, the ideal procedure is to give some good, quiet work on the trail or in the open country. However, if such off days become frequent, they indicate either that your training has not been successful or that your horse has a temperament that presents a problem. If your training is the fault, you should go back to work along the fence from a standstill and review the early stages of training to back. If the horse has a temperament that requires the use of force now and then, call in your helper and use the gate or the long pole to make the horse back. Then work him in the arena and insist that he back straight for a few steps. If necessary, your helper can assist from the ground. Do not continue to repeat any movement after you have gained your point, but you must persist until the horse obeys what he knows is demanded of him.

In any use of force in an argument you are having about backing, the one thing you must avoid is the "dead," or steady, pull on the reins. It is easily possible to ruin a young horse's mouth while you are teaching him to back. If you have taught your horse properly, he knows that the spoken word "Back" and a pull on the reins are the signal for him to step backward. If you want him to take several steps backward, it may be necessary to repeat the word and the definite little pulls. With some horses it is necessary to repeat these signals in rhythm with the backward steps. In some instances the little pulls have to be very sharp and definite, but they should not be prolonged into a lugging on the reins. Confine the use of your bit to its function as a signal. Do not use it as a means of punishment.

One final word of caution is this: Although your horse must be willing and able to take a few backward steps as he stops from any gait, you should not ask him to back each time he stops, because later on in his training a stop may be immediately followed by a quarter-turn or a rollback or some other movement.

MORE ON LEADS

As I mentioned earlier, before you try to teach your horse anything about leads, you yourself must become completely familiar with them and be able to recognize them instantly. Do this by first observing from the ground an experienced horseman who will tell you which lead his horse is on and will demonstrate a change of leads. Then you should mount the experienced horse and have the experienced horseman tell you which lead the horse has. You should work with this experienced horse and horseman until you can recognize the leads instantly when you are mounted.

Because the extremely fast trot is not a virtue in the Western horse in the show ring or elsewhere, he does not need to be taught that breaking from a trot or gallop is a mortal sin. In the Western pleasure classes and in trail classes, horses are asked to trot; but the trot required is at a speed natural for any horse at that gait. Very little schooling is required to teach him to hold a trot when he is asked to do so. Therefore it is permissible and sometimes very useful to trot a horse into his leads at the gallop. The horse that will not readily take the proper lead or one that tends to do a disunited gallop often has to be helped considerably by this procedure.

Before you can trot a horse into his lead at the gallop, you must learn to post well. In posting, your seat rises slightly from the saddle at every other step of the horse's trot. This means that your weight rhythmically shifts from seat to stirrups and back in rhythm with your horse's trot.

If you are posting the trot on a straightaway and push your horse on into a gallop, he almost invariably leads with the foot which has been striking the ground as your seat comes into the saddle in posting. In other words, you rise at the trot with the rise of the foot with which you do not want him to lead. So if you want a left lead at the gallop, you start by rising with the horse's right foot at the trot.

PREPARING FOR ROLLBACKS, PIVOTS, AND SPINS

For the horse that will readily take the inside lead on any turn and will do so without ever performing a disunited gallop, no preliminary work need be done before teaching him to do the rollback. However, with the horse that has any difficulty at all in his leads, a little work at trotting into the proper lead is a good preliminary for teaching the rollback.

From one side of the ring trot straight across the center toward the opposite side. As you do so, post by rising with the right forefoot of your horse. A few steps before you reach the opposite side, push your horse toward the gallop, so that he will break into the gallop just as you reach the opposite side, and turn him to the left. If you have done this properly, your horse will then be on the left lead at the gallop. If, for any reason, he is disunited or on the wrong lead, stop him and start over again. Of course, to get the left lead at the gallop, you start the trot by rising with his left forefoot and turning him to the right.

When your horse begins to get the idea of what is wanted but still hits a disunited gallop now and then, you can bring him out of it without stopping him. Do so by keeping his nose pulled slightly away from the side with which you want him to lead. At the same time, use your leg or heel behind the cinch on the side opposite the leading side. Use the leg aid smartly enough to give him a little burst of speed, and he will change leads behind. (In his disunited gallop, he is already on the proper lead in front.) What this means is that you have caused your horse to be on a diagonal to his line of progress, with his leading shoulder ahead of the other one, and you have given him a burst of speed; you will see this method used in show-ring classes of three- and five-gaited horses to correct a wrong lead as well as to correct a disunited "canter."

It is wise to continue the lessons at trotting into the proper lead at the gallop until both you and your horse can perform it with ease. Then you are ready to start on the rollback.

To start teaching the rollback, follow this procedure: Have your horse galloping around the ring or corral to the left. He will, of course, be on the left lead. When you are approaching a midway point of one side of the arena, drop him into a trot, and post the trot by rising with his left foreleg. Then, by turning him toward the *outside* of the arena, that is, to your right, reverse your direction and push him into a gallop as he completes the 180-degree turn.

The first few times you perform this maneuver you may have to give yourself a little room for the reverse turn; that is, you may have to come down the side of the arena a few yards away from the fence. What you will be performing these first few times will not be a true rollback. It will merely be reversing in a very small circle. However, learning to reverse in a small circle and come out with a change of lead is a good preliminary to learning the true rollback.

THE ROLLBACK

The horse that has a very good mouth and an excellent stop needs very little teaching to do the rollback. If yours is such a horse, you may, while galloping him around the arena to the left, stop him midway of one side of the arena, lift him slightly just as he completes his stop, and swing him in a complete reverse to the right, that is, toward the outside of the arena. As he is completing his reversal, push him into the gallop and he will come out on a right lead. It is very important that you do not start to turn him before he completes his stop. To do so, of course, will cause him to cross his forelegs and to be confused; but he must be put into the reverse turn while he is still collected from his stop, and he must be pushed into his gallop in the new direction just *as* he completes his reversal.

If your horse does not have the extremely light mouth and excellent stop that enables you to teach him the rollback in the manner I have just described, you will do well to continue trotting him into it for some time, gradually decreasing the amount of trotting and increasing the speed of the reverse turn. Finally you will be able to bring him to a quick stop and turn toward the outside of the arena into a complete reverse without describing a circle. Ultimately you will achieve the perfect rollback. This is the way it is done:

With some speed, you will gallop your horse down a straightaway on a right lead, let us say, stop him, lift him into a reverse turn to the left, and bring him out on a left lead.

In the show ring there are markers to indicate where the rollback is to be performed. However, at home in the training arena or corral it is not advisable, after the horse has learned what is wanted in the rollback, to perform this maneuver repeatedly in the same place, for he will learn to anticipate the rollback just as a horse will anticipate the stop if it is repeated again and again in the same place.

While we are considering the show ring, let us pause a moment to think about the matter of the position of the horse's head. As I mentioned earlier, considerable fuss is made over this business. Many a horse has been beaten over the head to make him conform to current fashion in head carriage. However, careful observation of top performers in the show ring teaches us that no good performer ducks his head when he stops or executes a rollback. Certainly no good horseman condones opening of the mouth or throwing up of the head on stopping or turning, but most good horses will raise their heads slightly when they stop or turn quickly.

If your horse tends to throw up his head, it may be necessary to work him for a while with a tiedown and a rope nose band. It is wise to examine closely what you are doing with your hands and your weight in the saddle to be sure that the cause of your problem is not on your end of the reins or on top of the saddle. Hands that jerk on the reins or that get too high at the wrong time will cause any horse to throw up his head. Getting weight too far back may not be a direct cause of a high head, but it increases the difficulty of fast stopping and thereby causes the rider to increase the intensity of everything he is doing to get the horse to stop. The poor beast is doing all it can to respond with its feet. Anything further must be done with the head, tail, or some other part of the anatomy. (You can keep the head down with a standing martingale; but up to now, no one has devised a gimmick to stop a wringing tail.)

In making the perfect reining horse there is no substitute for time, intelligent and patient work in communicating to the horse what is wanted, and the good sense to know when to insist and when to humor. The perfect golfer, dancer, or skater did not learn his skill in a day, certainly not in less than a year. Is your horse so far superior to such humans (possibly he is in integrity, but certainly not in understanding human demands) that he can learn faster? You may fake a good performance by the use of gimmicks and shorten the "training" period, but you will not have the perfection you strive for.

PIVOTS

The next movement to teach is the one that in 1968 is most commonly called the pivot. A few years ago it was called the offset, a name still used for it in some places. It is also called the quarter-turn. Probably fashion will decree another name for it soon. Whatever the name, it is a movement that will make you keep your horse's mouth light, and it is a movement that is required in reining and stock-horse classes in all shows. In the pivot, the horse is collected with his weight on his haunches. Then his forehand is lifted and turned 90 degrees to the right or left. His hind feet act as a pivot and move neither forward nor backward. His forefeet do not touch the ground between the moment he is lifted and the completion of the movement.

I like to start teaching the pivot by riding at a fairly collected gallop, the gait that usually passes for a canter in a five-gaited class. Riding this gallop along a fence, I bring the horse to as near a sliding stop as the speed affords. While he is still collected from the stop, I raise my hand slightly, or move it backward, depending upon which is necessary to lift the forehand without making the horse I am working toss his head in the air. As his forehand rises, I swing my hand to the side, away from the fence. When his forefeet touch ground, I slack my rein, say "Whoa," and stroke the horse on the neck to let him know he has done well.

At this first lesson, I certainly do not strive for a 90-degree turn—just a lift of the forequarters and a slight turn without moving his hind feet forward or backward. I do not even ask the horse to pivot back into the direction from which I turned him. One successful lift and turn is enough for the first day. Not until he gets the hang of the movement do I ask him to rise high enough in front to make a full quarter-turn. When he can do this, I ride him the opposite direction of the fence and ask him for a quarter-turn away from it. When he can give me a quarter-turn away from the line of progress along the fence going either direction, I ride him in a straight line down the middle of the arena and ask him for a quarter-turn to the left and a return quarter-turn to the right, so he ends the movement facing the direction toward which he was headed when he started it.

The most important part of teaching the pivot is to take plenty of time at the first lessons to make sure that the horse gets the idea of what is wanted and to enable the rider to determine just what to do with his hands and heels to get the horse to collect himself on his haunches sufficiently to lift his forehand off the ground and place his front feet to the side. An observer from the East remarked that what is done in this movement is overcollecting the horse and turning him to the side. However one wishes to view and label the movement, it must be executed without causing the horse to yaw his mouth open or throw his head in the air. The finished product of good training will pivot in response to signals so slight that they can scarcely be observed by an audience. To achieve this result, you must first of all have a light mouth on your horse. Then you must learn to collect him momentarily with a light lift or backward movement of the hand and a squeeze with your legs or light touch of the spur. Then all that is needed is to intensify the momentary collection—lift the forehand off the ground—and place the forefeet to the side.

It is extremely easy to sour a horse on this movement during the early lessons by repeating it too many times in one workout.

THE SPIN

The spin is a collection plus a complete 360-degree turn. In other words, it is four pivots in succession in the same direction. Because Western classes in shows are relatively new, requirements change, sometimes from year to year. I have seen classes in which horses were required to gallop at speed, slide, spin, and come out of the spin on a gallop in a new lead. This, of course, meant that the horse started his spin by turning to the side away from the one on which he was galloping. For the horse that has learned the rollback, this is not a great feat. In the rollback he has learned to do a 180-degree turn over his hocks and come out of it on a new lead. A careful trainer can readily teach him that what is wanted is a complete 360-degree turn before he takes off in a new lead.

If the requirement is for the horse to spin and come out on the same lead on which he was galloping before he started to spin, start the spin by turning toward the side on which he has been leading at the gallop. Before starting to teach your horse the spin from a gallop and sliding stop, teach him to do four pivots in succession in the same direction. This will mean, of course, that his hind feet act as a pivot, putting their imprints down within a circle of very small circumference. Some judges do not require that the hind feet work within such a small area. Some trainers allow the horse to bob up and down on the spin like a hobby horse, so his hind feet follow the tracks of his forefeet. One of the most famous of the performing Arabians in the 1930's would spin many times in succession, with his hind feet following the tracks of his forefeet, bobbing like a hobby horse while spinning like a top.

While the kind of spin I have just described makes a flashy spectacle, it has not yet been required in the show ring. The hobby-horse type of spin may satisfy some judges, but the spin on the hindquarters keeps the horse in proper balance to come out of the spin in a gallop on the proper lead.

FIGURE EIGHTS AND FLYING CHANGE OF LEADS

Any horse that can do a rollback, pivot, or spin needs scarcely any teaching to do a figure eight or to do a flying change of leads. We might even say that any horse that will invariably take the proper lead on any turn can do a figure eight. Any horse, unless he is extremely awkward or from the time of his foaling has always been confined in small quarters, will do a flying change of leads when he is running in a pasture. This means that if he is galloping on the left lead, let us say, and makes a quick turn to the right, he will change to the right lead. At the racetrack, running horses being asked for a burst of speed down the home stretch will often change to a new lead. There are various theories as to the reason for this, but the principal one is that the horse is tired on the lead on which he has been traveling.

Because the flying change of lead seems to be natural for the horse, some trainers use it much earlier in the training program than I have placed it here. They use it to correct the horse that is prone to do a disunited canter or gallop whenever he is asked for a change of lead. It is true that a burst of speed induced by a boot with the heel behind the cinch on the side opposite the one on which the horse is leading in front will usually correct a disunited gallop. On the cold-blooded or sluggish horse, this trick may be a very useful one. However, if a horse has much hot blood in him, this method of correcting the disunited gallop will excite him and usually add to his confusion. Because my chief concern in training a horse is to communicate to him what is wanted rather than to scare him or pain him into doing something accidentally, I prefer to work on the figure eight and the flying change after the horse has understood what I mean when I ask him for a change of lead.

To begin work on the flying change of leads, start the horse on a gallop with some speed to the left. This means, of course, that he is on the left lead. Just as you complete the turn, on one end of the arena or corral, head your horse in a straight line for the center of the corral or arena and continue that straight line diagonally across the arena so that you will have to turn to the right when you reach the opposite side. Just as you reach the opposite side and begin the turn to the right, ask your horse for a little more speed by using your left leg behind the cinch. Of course, if your horse is a bit sluggish, you will have to use heel or spur. Keep your weight well forward in the saddle and lean toward the *outside*. Your horse should respond, of course, by immediately changing to the right lead. If he doesn't, slow him down and stop him. Let him calm down and then try the whole operation over again. This time, when you start to turn to the right, asking for the change of lead, keep your horse's head slightly toward the outside, that is, toward the left. If he changes in front and does not change behind, use your left leg aid again and use it very sharply, asking for a considerable burst of speed. Be sure your weight is forward and that you are leaning toward the outside. If you find this difficult, remember that a horn on a saddle can be used for more purposes than just to hold a rope.

If your horse is one of those very rare ones that do not respond with a flying change of lead when handled in the manner I have just indicated, it is very important that *you* do not become excited. See to it that excitement and confusion are all confined below the saddle and on the front end of the reins. If your horse has plenty of hot blood and has become excited after two or three of your attempts to get him to do the flying change of lead, desist. Let him walk quietly. Take him out of the arena, if necessary, and do some work that he likes to do and that he knows well how to do. In short, do anything with him that will calm him down and quiet him. It may be wise not to try the flying change of lead again until another day.

After the horse has learned to do the flying change of leads in the figure eight, it is possible to get him to do a flying change on a straightaway. If you are galloping him on the left lead, for instance, in a straight line and turn him to the right, you will get a right lead. Eventually you will be able to get a flying change of leads merely by applying the leg aid on the side opposite the one on which the horse is leading. The execution of the flying change of lead calmly, smoothly, and pleasantly is a demonstration of the excellence of the horse's education and also of the horsemanship of the rider.

AIDS, BATS, AND BITS

To execute the kind of spin I prefer, you must, of course, keep your horse from flopping his hindquarters to the right when he is turning his forehand to the left in a spin, and vice versa when spinning in the opposite direction. If all your work with your horse has been good, you and he will be well acquainted with the leg aids. You will be riding both ends of your horse. So all you will need to do to keep his hindquarters working within a very small circle when he spins is to use your right leg well behind the cinch when spinning him to the left and your left leg when you are spinning to the right. He must move neither forward nor backward as he spins. If he tends to back up as he spins, you are probably using too much backward pull on your reins. Raise your hand a trifle and use less pressure. If this is not the remedy, you may need to use a little more impulsion with your legs or spurs.

While more harm is done by misuse of punishment and force on horses than there is good done by their proper use, there are horses, like children, that have to learn that they *must* do what is required of them whether they like it or not. The harm by the use of punishment or force is usually done by the trainer who lacks the skill of letting the horse know what is wanted, and also lacks the sensitivity to know when the horse is merely confused and when he is rebelling. Of course, the horse sometimes rebels because the trainer has run a good thing into the ground; he has overworked on one movement until he has soured his horse on it.

If you have a horse that understands what is wanted of him but slacks off on his work or rebels even though you have not soured him by overwork, do not use your spurs to punish him. A horse's sides can become "hard" just as his mouth can; and, of course, you must not spoil his light mouth by the use of your regular bit for punishment. Use a bat instead of spurs, whether the force is needed to give more impulsion or to control a sidewise movement of the quarters. With skill, the bat can also be used to command a swing to the side of the forehand. If the need for aid is in raising the forehand or restraint, try a gag rein. This device is a pair of reins fastened at the top of the bridle and run freely through the rings of a snaffle bit. The gag reins can be used only with lateral pulls—plow rein, not neck rein. If you are fortunate enough to have the friendship of a person of Spanish extraction who is a master of the use of the bosal (I mean the Baja California bosal that works on the lower jaw), he can show you a technique far more effective than the gag rein, one to which a considerable portion of my *Out of the West* is devoted. However, use of this bosal is an art that cannot be learned quickly, so the gag rein is the preferable remedy. Its effectiveness is championed by one of the foremost trainers of barrel horses today. She even goes so far as to say that one of the first things to do in training is to get the corners of a horse's mouth a bit sore by the use of the gag rein. Obviously, I am not in complete agreement with her, but as a remedy in special cases, her method is good.

With the gag rein used as correction, you cannot keep your horse's head from going skyward unless you use a standing martingale; but when the war is over, you may go back to your regular bit and gradually loosen the tiedown until you finally dispense with it.

Once you are sure of the need for force, don't be halfhearted about it. Use the bat with exact timing and make it talk (the sound of the bat is a major part of its effectiveness). Don't lug on the gag reins. Make sure your pulls on them are as quick and hard as is necessary to get results. If necessary, your sharp, definite pulls may be given in rapid and prolonged succession. When you have gained your point, whatever it may be, don't become so elated that you keep on repeating whatever movement it is that you are correcting. The war is not over, and tomorrow you may have to repeat your job, but don't sour your horse in one day's work.

A case in point is the final ride of my friend who was a trainer on the RO ranch near Sonoita, Arizona, some years ago. He was correcting a very hot-blooded horse that had been running past the calf in roping. My friend had gained his point and was just ready to put his horse away when his wife drove up with some guests. To entertain the guests, my friend asked his wife to let out one more calf. His horse that had performed perfectly on the last two calves started to veer off course and pass the calf. When reprimanded by his rider, the horse, to quote one of the guests, "exploded straight up into the air and came to earth upside down on top of his rider," who lived less than an hour.

Had that hot-blooded horse been put away when my friend first started to take him out of the arena, he probably would have worked satisfactorily the next day. As my friend well knew, the horse was hot and his nerves were strung up. He had had about all he could take and under severe compulsion had finally performed as told. That was the time to let him stop work.

8

THE ROPE HORSE

In the days before nylon ropes, horse trailers, and professional rodeos, teaching a horse to work a rope was often a rough business. One way to do it was to rope a big, wild steer, step away, and let the horse and steer battle the situation out. Some thirty years ago I witnessed a variation of this method. The variant was the rock wall of a corral on the 88 Ranch, near Superior, Arizona.

A little bunch of rather wild cattle had been brought down from the "hills" and hazed into a rock corral. One roan steer had made so much trouble on the way down by cutting back toward home that a rope bridle and snaffle bit had been put on him, and the bit was fastened by a short rope to one of his forelegs. This caused his trip to be somewhat laborious, and the fight should have been pretty well out of him by the time he was corraled. In the corral, he was roped and the rigging taken off him. When turned loose, he threw up his head, snorted, and surveyed the fence for a low spot. One of the hands spotted him. It may have been Dillard Pittman, for he was a good man with a rope and knew what a steer was going to do before the steer made up his mind. Dillard was riding a rather green horse that had tried his patience several times that day. Whoever the hand was, he was no greenhorn, for just as that roan *orejano* cleared the low spot in the wall, a rope settled neatly over his horns. The rider stepped away, and when the slack went out of that rope, both steer and horse went kerflop on the ground. They both got to their feet at the same time, and the battle was on. By the time that pony had the steer choked down, he had learned a lot about working a rope, and he never forgot it.

This method was a bit costly, for sometimes a steer would

break its neck as it reached the end of the rope in one of its rushes past the dodging horse. Occasionally a horse would break a leg. Of course, the steer could be butchered or skinned, but there isn't much salvage in a horse with a broken leg.

The methods of putting a stop on a horse (teaching him to stop) were various, but many of them were as violent as the one just described for rope work. The use of the draw rein and snaffle could leave about as obvious a testimonial on the horse as any. Two old geldings in my corral are cases in point. Both have mutilated tongues. In one of them, the end of the tongue is attached to the back part by a piece of flesh no larger in diameter than your finger, but the old boy can still catch a calf—and does he stop! I was told that the rider who used the draw rein that cut the old boy's tongue was fearful that the horse would die from loss of blood the day he learned to stop; Western horses of his breed are tough. The gelding is now quite long in the tooth but as hale and hearty as any two-year-old.

Fortunately, not all horsemen of pre-jet days were given to the violent practices I've just mentioned. Many of the best horses of that day were first used for a year or two on a hackamore, leading pack mules to distribute salt on the range, or used as transportation by hands checking siphons at watering places or mending fence. Now and then, one such hand might come across an animal that needed doctoring or a calf that had been missed at branding time. Such a critter would be brought in to the home corral or roped and attended to on the spot. This gave the young horse a taste of handling stock. When the youngster was put to actual stock work, he was eased into it, and allowance was made for his inexperience. Young humans growing up on such ranches learned to "make a hand" (become an expert cowboy) in a very similar manner. A boy would start swinging a rope almost as soon as he could toddle. Soon, no dog, duck, chicken, or goose of the door yard was safe from his noose. As he grew into a saddle, he had to be threatened with the dire consequences of unnecessarily roping range stock, and he surreptitiously roped it whenever he could. When he was finally put to work at roundup time, allowances were made for him.

Horses and boys deprived of the great (and usually unappreciated) privilege of growing up "the natural way" on such a ranch have to learn to become cowponies and cowboys by a more artificial method, usually a shorter one.

THE MODERN ROPING HORSE

If a horseman lives a long time and sees many horses, he may see one or two that are good mounts for all kinds of roping—calf roping (and tying), steer roping of single steers (called "busting" or "tripping"), team roping, and any other kind that comes along. However, the horse that is an expert at one kind of roping is usually confused and often unsuitable for other kinds of roping.

In the 1930's, before the term "Quarter Horse" was known in Arizona (horses of the type now designated by that term were called "Steel Dusts" then), the officials and guards at the state prison at Florence, Arizona, prided themselves on their fine privately owned mounts and on the pack of hounds owned by the state, used to track down escapees and lost persons. One of the guards paid more than he could afford for a very fine RO stallion. The RO on a horse in those days was as significant as the mark "sterling" on a piece of silverware. Few of them were seen off the vast spread of the Green Cattle Company, which then straddled the Mexican border for many miles, because that outfit, like many others, was averse to having its brand scattered about. A horse wearing the RO brand off the ranch was suspect (as a stolen horse) unless his rider was a well-known friend of the company. The guard was proud of his mount, not only because of the distinction of riding an RO but also because soon it had become apparent that it was one of the best calf-roping horses in Pinal County.

The fall that followed the pride was rather tragic. Team roping was becoming a popular diversion for officials at the prison. Like golf, team roping, especially heeling, can be fun for men a bit long in the tooth, who are not quite up to the speed of calf tying. The prison doctor and the warden enjoyed the sport (explained later in this chapter) and urged the guard to participate with his fine RO stallion. On a beautiful Sunday afternoon the doctor persuaded him to head a steer, which the physician would heel. The RO broke from the box and was on the steer in three strides.

His rider made a perfect catch, but the steer's heels were never presented to the doctor. That calf horse knew that when a rope whizzed over his ears, he must stop, and stop he did. No jab of spur or yank of bit could make him go on and turn off after the steer's head was roped. The guard, embarrassed and angry, punished the horse severely and made two or three more tries that afternoon. Next day, alone, he tried to "teach" the horse to work properly as a header. All he succeeded in doing was to arouse the horse's anger and create confusion. From then on, that fine animal was no good as a calf horse or as a steer horse.

Florence, Arizona, was also the home of one of the only three horses I have ever known to be top performers at all kinds of roping. He was a gift to James Heron, sheriff of Pinal County, from one of the top rodeo stars of the day by the name of Knight. The horse was a dark-bay gelding with a star and a white sock. Star wasn't very big, about one thousand pounds, and he was built like the good old Hambletonians, not all "kicked up in a pile," as some old-timers used to describe the early, bulldog-type Quarter Horses. In one afternoon at Casa Grande, Arizona, I saw him used to win a calf-roping event and used twice in team tying, once by the header and once by the heeler; and one of those teams won the money. Steer "busting" was not permitted in Arizona rodeos at that time, but I saw Star carry his rider to victory in a contest of "busting" by several cowboys on a little ranch outside Superior, Arizona. The other participants rode big horses far more suitable for "busting" than Star.

It was interesting to see "Little Jim," as the sheriff's son was called, allow his horse to compensate for his lack of size and weight. The other riders would turn their horses at right angles as soon as the steer's head was roped, and the rope flipped over his hips to pull against his hind legs just above the hocks. Little Jim gave Star the slack as he overhauled the steer. He was a good roper and had the head roped and the slack around the hind legs seemingly all in one movement. As the rope hit the steer's hind legs, Star gained speed and shot straight ahead, flopping the steer in a backward somersault into the air and onto the ground on its back. The steer undoubtedly weighed at least three-fourths as much as the horse, but Star made up in speed and finesse for his lack of weight.

Another exception to the rule lived and worked the range out of Superior. He was the top horse of Wayne Taylor, whose range at that time extended from high in the mountains above Superior to a ten-square-mile "pasture" just outside Florence. Wayne

Pima, the most efficient and versatile stock horse (roping and cutting) the author has ever seen. The late Wayne Taylor (dismounted) operated one of Arizona's largest ranches. (From an old snapshot taken by the author's father.)

bought the horse from the Pima Indians for seven dollars and gave him their name. Pima never saw a rodeo, and if Wayne had ever seen anyone using the little blaze-faced bay in a contest, homicide would undoubtedly have ensued. Though Wayne had accounted well for himself in a few rodeos before I knew him and could be persuaded to do a little team tying after that time, he would not hire a hand that had any rodeo aspirations and would not use Pima in a contest. He wanted his cattle handled as quietly as possible, though on one little pocket of his mountain range, where the cattle could go two years without seeing man or horse, "quiet handling" had to be interpreted very liberally.

I have seen Pima insinuate himself quietly into a bunch of eighty or a hundred cows and calves just brought down from the hills and maneuver into a position where Wayne could rope a calf without stirring up the herd. I have seen him drag a calf to the branding fire, pivot, and back up on the rope to hold it while the two hands at the fire could work on their jobs of ear marking, tail bobbing, branding, vaccinating, and castrating. One very hot late afternoon, Pima backed up on the rope, holding the calf still for the hands to work on it. Wayne, hot and thirsty, dismounted, walked to an olla hanging on a mesquite limb one hundred feet away, got himself a cool drink, and returned to remount Pima, who was still quietly holding the rope taut.

Some of the cattle, those from one little pocket in the mountains called Haunted Canyon, were very shy, so shy that I once saw one of them clear a six-foot rock wall when a stranger approached the opposite side of the corral and peered over the wall. Pima could cut an animal out of a bunch of those *orejanos* without raising dust. He would also, when cutting cattle that were sluggish, grab an animal with his teeth at the root of its tail and instantly convert it to the belief that it should go in the way he directed.

Pima could offset (quarter-circle), pivot, rollback, side pass, and do any other movement currently fashionable in the show ring better than most show horses; but neither he nor his owner knew the names of those movements, and I doubt seriously that they knew the "correct" signals for them. The little bay was a good horse at the head or at the heels of a steer. More than once I saw him and another horse of the Taylor outfit quickly stretch out a bull weighing much more than either horse; yes, almost as much as both of them, for neither weighed one thousand pounds.

Horses capable of becoming as versatile as Star and Pima are as rare as are humans capable of becoming Winston Churchills. So it is wise to pick a horse with the qualifications suitable for a given type of work and then train him for that one type of work.

THE CALF-ROPING HORSE

Calf roping demands skill of the rider and of the horse. Many ropers assert that the skill of the horse is more important for success than the skill of the rider. Certainly it is at least a fifty-fifty affair, although much of the skill of the rider is beyond the scope of this book. Jerking the slack, throwing it away, going down the rope, legging or flanking, and tying are skills without which the perfect horseman on the perfectly trained horse cannot succeed in calf roping. For a brief but excellent discussion of those skills, I refer the reader to a little book called *Calf Roping*, written by Toots Mansfield, published by *The Western Horseman*, 3850 North Nevada Avenue, Colorado Springs, Colorado. It is available at the Wm. N. Porter Saddle Shop, 6048 North 16th Street, Phoenix, Arizona, and at other saddle shops in the West and at some book stores.

The important skills of the rope horse can be listed under five headings: (1) performing properly in the box, (2) scoring, (3) rating, (4) stopping, and (5) working the rope.

PERFORMANCE IN THE BOX

Many a fast rope horse has been ruined in the box. The rider that jams his mount back against the pole at the rear of the box and then hangs on to the reins to hold him there starts a chain reaction. Such a rider usually uses a cable nose band, a short tiedown, or a "severe" bit (though any bit is severe if the hand on the rear end of the reins is bad). The torture of the bit pulling the head up and the wire cable on the soft nose holding it down, plus the bred-in urge to go forward, build up a head of steam that is bound to explode. If, in his frantic threshing from side to side and up and down, the horse manages somehow to rear in spite of the tiedown, the rider beats him over the head. After a little of such treatment, any horse (especially if he has enough thoroughbred blood in him to give him the speed so necessary in a calf-roping horse) is impossible to keep quiet in a box.

The alternative to such treatment of the horse difficult to handle in the box is, as suggested elsewhere in this chapter, lots of time spent going into and from the box casually, without cattle.

This plus practice, a little later, at standing in the box while cattle are let out will help. However, with the highly bred, nervous horse, the handling of the reins is very important. On such a horse any steady pull on the reins while in the box is cause for trouble. If he moves forward, a short, sharp, and very definite pull on the reins will restrain him. Such a pull may have to be lightning swift, and the release of pressure must be equally swift. Though such a "snatching back" is successful, the next instant the horse will again start forward. Again he must be restrained with the deft, sharp, quick pull, instantly released.

This use of the reins has been called "shaking" the reins. It is a technique that demands skill. Inept attempts at it frequently result in ill-timed jerks on the reins that punish the mouth and irritate the horse without any desirable effect whatever; or they result in a jiggling of the reins that serves no purpose other than to increase the horse's excitement. Nevertheless, the only way the hot-blooded, excitable horse can be taught to work properly in the box is to place him where he belongs; then, the moment he steps out of position, pull him instantly back to where he belongs. If the next moment he steps out again, pull him back—and so on. The pulling is done by a deft wrist, not by the entire arm. Sometimes that wrist must act like spring steel.

Patience and time in getting the horse used to the noises and excitement of his job very gradually will result in teaching the most excitable horse to stand in the box.

Any time spent in teaching the rope horse to be calm in the box before you start to teach him to follow a calf is well spent. The more hot blooded and excitable the horse, the more time should be so spent. Begin by getting him to enter the box calmly and willingly. If the horse is an exceedingly nervous and excitable one, it may even be wise simply to lead him into the box on a halter and allow him to eat a little feed, which you have placed in the back corner of the box beforehand. Spend days, if necessary, simply riding him into the box, allowing him to stand for a few minutes, and riding him out. Ride him out first on a walk; gradually you will be able to bring him out on a trot or a gallop. As soon as he is perfectly calm about going into the box and coming out, get a helper to make a little noise in the chute while the horse is standing in the box. The amount and duration of racket (shaking the gate and kicking the fence boards) in the chute that is advisable the first few times depends upon the temperament and the response of the horse. Let him find out that nothing that happens in the chute is harmful to him.

When this has been accomplished, let several calves leave the chute while you keep the horse standing quietly in the box. When the horse takes this calmly, it is time to begin to allow him to come out of the box and follow the calf. For the first few times he does this, do not try for any speed. Work up to scoring very gradually. (The term "scoring" means getting to the calf as quickly as possible when signaled to do so.)

No matter how carefully you have prepared your horse for his work in the box, problems are likely to arise after you start the actual work of roping calves. It is difficult to keep the horse from anticipating; that is, any rattling of the gate or other noise in the chute causes him to attempt to lurch out of the box. The obvious remedy for this, of course, is to let out a few calves without allowing him to follow them. With a high-strung horse, this should be done rather frequently. Get a helper to rattle the gate and to pop it open a few times while the horse remains in the box.

Another common fault that develops early in some horses is rearing in the box. The sight of a rearing horse being beaten over the head in a box is all too common. Certainly he should not be beaten over the head with a rope, for this will make him shy of a rope. If you acquire a horse that has this habit, he certainly must be broken of it. If you must hit him over the head, keep a short piece of rubber hose handy by the box and use it instead of your rope or a club.

The ideal way to place a rope horse in the box is to ride him into the box alongside the chute. When you reach the back of the box, turn him away from the chute and place him in the back corner of the box in the side away from the chute, pet him, and settle him down. This ideal is reached, however, only by those horses that have been very carefully handled.

Among horses that will stand when properly placed in the box, many will drive their hind legs into the back of the box with the takeoff. The remedy for this varies with the horse. With some it can be stopped by backing the horse solidly against the back of the box; others do better if they are moved a little farther forward in the box. Even though the ideal place for the horse in the box is on the side away from the chute, because from that point he can most quickly see the calf, it is advisable with many horses to shift position if the horse begins to show a tendency to lean against the side of the box. The cause of almost any problem with a roping horse's performance is the formation of undesirable habits. Because of this, you should watch your rope horse very carefully for any sign that you are the cause of his forming a bad habit.

SCORING

The term "scoring" is used for two different meanings. It may mean simply getting to the calf as soon as possible after it is out of the chute. The term is also used to indicate allowing a calf to cross a scoring line in front of the chute before the roper is allowed to cross the barrier. If your horse has formed the habit of taking to a calf the instant it is out of the chute, he will probably give you some trouble when you find yourself in a contest in which the calf is allowed an eight- or ten-foot start before it is legal for you to cross the barrier. The score line for a calf is usually some eight or ten feet outside the chute. This, of course, gives ample time for a horse to break the barrier and be penalized. So it is wise to work your horse at home so that he forms the habit of starting out of the box at *your* signal.

The speed with which your horse gets on the calf is of vital importance. It is possible that you may have to use your spur to increase his speed. However, be sure that whatever you use to increase the speed of scoring is not overused. The horse that anticipates the pain of the spur or flailing rope the moment the calf is released is usually a problem in the box.

RATING

The horse scores to get you to the calf, and he rates the calf by keeping you in the position you desire for throwing. He must keep you in that position no matter how the calf dodges or increases and decreases its speed.

It is up to you to determine the position that is best for you for throwing. This may very possibly be close to the calf, with your horse's head almost touching its hip. If so, that's where the horse should put himself when he scores. And that is where he should remain until you throw your rope. If your horse scores well and you are a good roper, he will need considerable extra work on rating. After you have roped two or three calves in good time, allow your horse to follow the next few calves for some distance before you rope them. It may take considerable practice before your horse learns to rate calves properly. Your timing will have to be excellent in the use of your spur when he lags and the use of your reins when he gains speed. Rating a calf is so important that you must teach your horse to do it well. If you become so engrossed in beating the stopwatch every time you practice, you may soon have a horse that will not rate a calf. It will pay off to forget the stopwatch occasionally when you are practicing and to concentrate on perfecting the horse's rating.

STOPPING

The throwing of your rope is a warning to your horse, not a signal to stop. As soon as your loop is over the calf's head, you must jerk the slack to prevent the calf from running through your loop. The instant the loop is jerked tight, you throw the slack away. You throw it up in front of your horse. This serves two purposes. It prevents the slack from getting fouled up in your gear, and it is an important part of your signal to your horse for the stop. The rest of that signal is the putting of your left hand on his neck and shifting your weight onto your left stirrup. The first few times you rope on your horse, you will, of course, need to signal him with your reins as you toss the slack in front of him, press on his neck with your left hand, and shift your weight onto your left stirrup. This is the moment when it is very easy to ruin what might have been a good rope horse. If you are excited and yank too severely on the reins, causing unnecessary pain, you will soon have a horse that does not wait until you throw the slack before he stops. He will soon be anticipating that pain on his mouth and will set all four feet and toss his head high in the air the moment you throw your rope. Take plenty of time to teach him to stop. Increase the quickness of his stopping gradually.

Calf roper Dave Eastlake at Prescott Rodeo. Note rope tossed ahead of horse and arm on neck—signals for a stop. *Photo courtesy Ben Allen, Rodeo Photos, Pasadena, California*

WORKING THE ROPE

The horse that works the rope properly faces the calf constantly and keeps the rope taut. The excellent horse will begin to back and to pull the calf toward the roper who is going down the rope toward the calf. However, it is equally important for the horse to stop backing at the moment the roper reaches the calf (and the calf reaches the roper as it is being dragged) and starts to flank or leg it.

If you have given the horse the training outlined in this book for the reining horse, he knows how to stop by voice and rein signal; he knows how to back straight and how to turn while backing in response to leg aid (which will enable you to straighten him if he tends to veer off to the side when backing on a rope). Also, because of your early work, you will be able to communicate to your horse what you want of him in the box. Because you can ride both ends of him, you can place your horse in the box with much more ease than can the rider mounted on a green horse that has not had the benefit of good early training. Because you have given your horse a good mouth and have made him responsive to leg aids, you can rate your horse more easily than the rider with a less well-trained mount. The one thing that will be entirely new to him in roping is working the rope. However, the good mouth you have so carefully given him and his responsiveness to the leg aids when backing will make your work in teaching him to work the rope a much easier job than it is for the man working with a horse that has not had as much education as yours.

To start teaching your horse to work a rope, get a sandbag that is heavy enough to offer about the same resistance to being dragged as will the weight of the calf. Your job is to teach the horse to drag the sandbag backward on command and to back in a straight line. With the horse that has not had good early training, this is often very difficult, especially if there is no long narrow lane in which to teach him. Usually the rider's patience is exhausted, the horse is confused, and a fight ensues. However, since you can communicate exactly what is wanted by rein, voice, and leg signals, your job is relatively simple. Fasten the rope to the sandbag, mount your horse, and dally (a gringo corruption for the Spanish phrase meaning to take a turn) the rope around the horn.

Back your horse in a straight line until the sandbag moves a few inches. If the first movement of the bag frightens your horse, release the dally, dismount, and lead your horse up to the bag. Holding the horse by the reins, touch the bag with your hand. Then sit on it. Communicate to the horse the harmlessness of the sandbag. When he seems convinced, move the bag slightly. If this startles him, take plenty of time to let him find out that it is harmless. When you can drag the bag toward the horse without frightening him, you are ready to remount. This time you can take the slack out of your rope before you start to back. As with every other new stunt, don't try too much at the first lesson. In another day or two you will be able to drag the sandbag in a straight line as far as you wish, while your horse keeps his face toward the bag and his body in a straight line with the rope.

The next step is to work from the ground. Have a foul rope on your horse. This is a rope around his neck just tight enough so that it will not come more than halfway back on his neck (toward his withers). With some horses it works best if it is tight enough to keep it from getting more than a few inches from his throttle. Fasten your rope to the saddle horn and pass the loose end through the foul rope. Standing a few feet in front of your horse, facing him, take the slack out of your lariat with your right hand and coil the surplus in your left hand. The moment you pull on your lariat, the horse may think you want him to come toward you. He may think this is a new way of leading him. If a voice signal does not cause him to stand still, you may have to stand a little closer to him when you pull the slack out of your lariat so you can reach his bridle and induce him to stand still. When he learns to stand still while you give tugs on the lariat, gradually step backward until you are tugging on the end of your lariat.

After your horse learns to stand still and face you while you give tugs on the lariat, give him the voice signal to back. If he doesn't immediately respond, a little flip on the rope may induce him to take the backward step. If this does not work, tie a metal ring on the front of your saddle. Have your bridle reins short enough so they will not come farther back than the front of your horse's withers. Then tie a clothesline to the end of those reins. Run it through the ring on the front of your saddle and thence to your hand. Now when you step back to the end of your lariat, give the voice signal to back and at the same time pull on the clothesline sharply. As soon as your horse will back in response to the voice signal without the aid of the clothesline, fasten your lariat to the sandbag and teach him to drag it backward in a straight line again for a time or two. As soon as your horse will drag the bag backward whenever you tell him to, stand halfway between the bag and your horse; tell him to back; and when he has dragged the bag to your feet, bend over it and tell the horse "Whoa!" If he does not stop backing when you tell him to, you may have to use the clothesline again, but this time attach it to the nose band or the bit of your bridle and run it from that point directly to your hand so that you can pull forward on the bridle when you tell him "Whoa."

When your horse has learned to drag the sandbag backward until it reaches your feet and then stop, it is time to mount him while he is standing still and the lariat is attached to the bag. Step off and tell your horse to back. As he starts to back, you start down the rope toward the bag. When you and the bag meet, tell your horse to stop. This is an important maneuver, and he must learn to do it well.

The next step in training is to teach your horse to continue facing the end of the rope no matter where it goes. Obviously, the way to do this is for you to get on the end of the rope and move from side to side. In this lesson, the foul rope will turn your horse's head toward the end of the rope. However, if he is a bit sluggish about turning, you may use a large cable nose band and a tiedown (standing martingale). Run your lariat through the cable nose band instead of through the foul rope for a few lessons. Gradually increase the speed of your movements on the end of the lariat until your antics come as close to simulating those of a live calf as your gymnastic ability will permit. Finally you can ask your horse to back while you are putting pressure on the rope and moving about from side to side. Put as much pressure on the rope as you can and move about as swiftly as possible so that the horse will be prepared for his work on a calf.

One trick, used by at least one of the top trainers, may help with the horse that has not had a preliminary education to make him attentive and responsive to human demands. It is this: Tie a second rope to the sandbag. Tie the other end of the rope to a solid post. The rope should be long enough so that there are a few coils of slack between the bag and the post. Start the horse backing. Time your movement so that you reach the sandbag and bend over it just as the slack is out of the rope attached to the post. If your ropes are good and the post is solid, the horse will stop and, usually, stand braced against the pull of the rope.

Whatever method is used, all signals for stopping except your bending over the sandbag must be gradually diminished and finally dispensed with before the horse is ready to work calves. When your rope is finally jerked tight around a calf's neck and you toss the slack, your horse must automatically stop, drag the calf toward you, and stop again when you bend over to leg or flank it. And he must do all of this without voice signal from you.

It may be objected that the method I have outlined takes too much time. But I call the attention of any objector to the price that can be had for a good rope horse. I also call attention to the scared and jerky performance of many horses in top contests. Such horses, when the roper has tied his calf and approaches preparatory to mounting and leaving the arena, shy and give other indications of terror indicative of past use of electric prods, beatings over the head, and other shortcuts in training. The horse that works confidently and smoothly usually puts his rider on the calf faster and helps him more in all other ways than does the frightened horse.

The performance of the rope horse, like the performance of horses in other fields, can be helped or hindered by the rider. The roper does not need to be cautioned about keeping his weight forward when he is after a calf, for he rises in his short stirrups and leans toward the calf. However, he will do well to consider his method of dismounting.

When you dismount, your horse's hind feet are well forward in his square stop. Most probably momentum will keep your weight over those hind feet, but if you are tall and active, there is a possibility that you may swing too far up and back as you dismount. Keep your left hand well forward as it presses on your horse's neck (a signal to him to stop) and the elbow of your right arm crooked as your right hand grabs the horn to dismount. Bend your right knee and keep it low over the cantle and close to your horse as it comes down. As that right leg starts down, flip your left foot out of the stirrup and reach with it for the ground. Your left foot, taking your first forward stride, will absorb and use some of the momentum.

If you swing wide away from your horse when you dismount, you may swing him off balance. If you try to stop the momentum of your body by putting it all into your left stirrup as you dismount, you may tangle your own feet as you hit the ground. Most certainly you will throw your horse off balance unless you are extremely light and he is big and handy. Practice dismounting from a sliding stop as faithfully as you practice with your pigging string [braided rope used to tie calf's feet].

9

THE STEER HORSE

The unorthodox title above covers all uses of the horse for roping steers, both orthodox and unorthodox.

In recognized rodeos and shows today, with the exception of those in three states, steer "busting," tripping, or flipping is not permitted. However, where it is practiced today, it is done a little differently from the old-time method common when wild cattle ran on unfenced range.

In those days, according to one old-timer, the cowboy, with his rope tied hard and fast, would overtake a renegade, rope it by the horns or neck, toss the slack over the hips so that it pulled across the hind legs just above the hocks, turn about forty-five degrees to the left, and increase his speed. When the horse hit the end of the rope, if cinches and rope held, the steer would flip high in the air in a backward somersault and land hard enough on his back to knock himself into docility for a moment, usually long enough for the cowboy to get to him and hog-tie him before the animal came to its senses.

Most steer jerking today is done not with the rope tied hard and fast, but with it dallied around the horn. When the steer is roped, the slack is flipped to come across his hind legs, the rope is dallied, and the horse is turned at a sharp right angle away from the steer. This does not cause the high backward somersault of the old method and it requires weight and size in the rope horse rather than extreme speed.

In the early days, especially in the Southwest, horses used on the range were small. I have seen a little 850-pound cowpony make a 1,000-pound steer take off skyward in a somersault that broke its neck on landing. Today we rather frown on breaking steers' necks, especially in public displays; so we use the big horses and roll the steers over on their sides.

Team roping is by far the most popular method of roping steers in our rodeos today. It is fast becoming more popular, for youngsters not quite old enough to wrestle a calf can heel a steer, and

Edwards and White team roping at Prescott Rodeo. *Photo courtesy Ben Allen, Rodeo Photos, Pasadena, California*

men past the age of breaking records in calf roping can also acquit themselves creditably with a heel rope.

If there is any disadvantage to this form of sport with a rope, it is that the best results demand a rather special horse. He must be big but he must also be handy, and he must be experienced enough to be very steady. Needless to say, he must also have a pretty good burst of speed; and at the same time, if he is to be used for heeling, he must be very easy to rate (amenable to the control of his speed).

Some of the best horses for team roping are good old ranch horses that have been used for the entire variety of work on a cattle ranch, though they may not be top-performing specialists at any one type of work. One authority on the subject who defi-

1

2

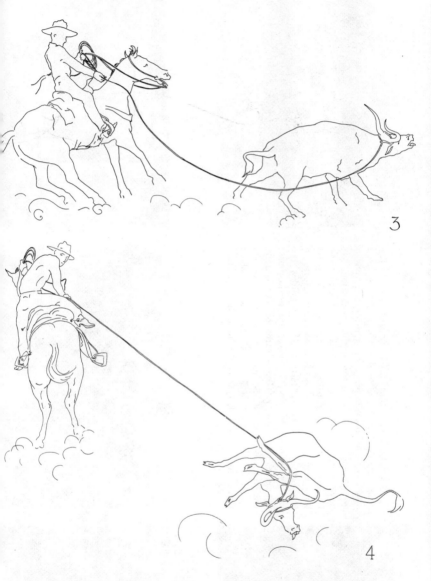

1. Steer buster casting loop. 2. Taking up the slack. 3. Flipping rope to right side of steer and starting to turn horse to left. 4. Increasing speed and busting steer.

4

5

1. Al Whiteman at Mountain View Stables in Scottsdale, Arizona, starting a good calf-roping horse on a new career of team roping. Al is using improvised equipment. The horse, a son of the great King, has never before been driven. 2. Al starts by letting the horse feel the drag of a log. 3. Horse is confused by long lines. 4. A helper is used to communicate to the horse what is wanted. 5. Helper guides the horse in starting to turn. 6. Helper guides the horse in completing turn. 7. Horse learns to start quietly without assistant at his head. 8. Horse learns to work the log without assistant at his head. 9. More work. 10. Horse has learned to hold the rope taut while standing still.

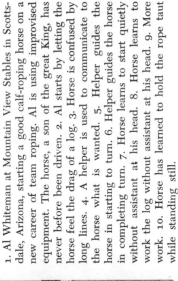

3

1

2

8

6

7

10

9

nitely states that the proper weight of a steer horse is from 1,125 to 1,250 pounds in working condition, says, "Don't worry about leads, but have him so you can rein him where you want him."

My very firm conviction is that the horses our friend uses have learned the hard way to change leads all by themselves at the proper times and to be always on the lead requisite for the work of the instant. If they hadn't so learned, they would not still be doing business.

"LOGGING" THE TEAM ROPING HORSE

The job of the horse ridden by the header is to wait quietly but ready for action in the box until the steer scores (crosses a designated line in front of the chute), then to put his rider in the place he prefers for roping, and to keep him there until he ropes the steer's head. As soon as the head is roped, the horse must turn the steer to the left at a right angle to the direction in which he was traveling when roped. As the heeler makes his catch, the header dismounts, and his horse must proceed in a straight line and continue his pull on the rope, *using the exact amount of pull* necessary to stretch the steer for throwing but not enough to drag the steer and heeling horse forward. This job of the heading horse working on his own is certainly not the most spectacular one in a rodeo. But when it is done right, it is, to me, the most admirable equine performance in the show. It calls for precision of power and something that looks more like judgment than we have a right to expect from a horse. It is *comparatively* easy to teach a horse to pull a moving object (please note the "comparatively"), but to teach him to modify that pull precisely at the instant it increases—modify it and sustain it sufficiently to keep the object stationary—that takes both equine and human intelligence. You can't beat, prod, gouge, or gimmick a horse into such a performance in a few weeks. And you can't teach that performance to a hothead or a dullard. You must have a good sensible horse to start with.

The process of teaching this performance is called "logging." The first step is, of course, to teach the horse to drive. Putting it in such words is sacrilege to the cowboy, so if you want to teach your horse to be a heading horse and your pride will not permit you to admit you are driving him, get a couple of long cotton ropes, tie a large ring to each hind cinch strap a few inches above the cinch buckle, put the ropes through them, and attach one end of each rope to a side of the bit. Get behind that horse and teach him to start, stop, and stand at verbal command (being careful never to move him faster than a walk). If you can't communicate by clucking that you want him to start, get a light fishing pole or a buggy whip. Use neither the whip nor the bit to inflict pain. Just a touch with the whip to tell him to start, and only enough pull on the reins to tell him to stop. Always use the voice signal at the same time you use the reins or the whip, and never move faster than a walk at this stage. If after many days your driving animal is sluggish about responding, a sharp pull on the reins to stop or a smart tap with the whip to start may be necessary. If you do use your whip, be sure your rope lines are long enough to allow you to stay out of range of the heels that may respond to that whip. Plenty of stopping and never twice in the same spot in one lesson is the rule for lessons at this stage.

The next step is to teach your horse to pull. With some horses it is advisable to start with a light log just heavy enough not to bounce onto his heels when he is walking. However, if your horse is very steady and sensible, you may start at once with something as heavy as a railroad tie. Make a fairly large honda with a bowline knot. Have it large enough so that you can easily slip it off the horn if your horse starts to tangle up in the rope. Have a chain or expendable piece of rope on the log.

A digression is in order here. One horseman whose skill and word I respect disagrees strongly with the usual method of teaching a steer horse to pull and to hold tension on the rope when standing still. Here is his word on the starting of training in pulling:

I pick for a steer horse a good old ranch horse. He knows what spurs and bit mean. I know most steer ropers teach a horse to pull and hold just the way they'd teach a workhorse to work in timber, but with a good ranch horse they're throwing away a lot of know-how that way, and maybe asking for a lot of confusion and fight.

I start an old horse from his back. Of course, the rope fastened to the log comes across my upper leg pretty tight when he pulls. But I'm not afraid of being pinned to the saddle, because I've picked me a good steady horse and we're not going to get into any whingding.

That horse knows he's to move forward when spurs or heels touch his side, whether there is something tied to the horn or not; so learning to pull a tie is no trick for him. The hardest thing to get into a horse's head is to keep that rope taut when he stops. That's where being in the saddle instead of on the ground is such an advantage. If you're on the ground, that horse will naturally ease up on the pull when you stop him. Then you use a whip. He jumps forward. You yank on the reins. Both you and the horse get mad.

When you're on the saddle and stop the horse, of course he'll ease up on the pull just the same as he would if you were on the ground behind him, *but* when you're on top of him you can squeeze him just enough with your legs or just touch him enough with your spurs to get him to lean into that rope.

As soon as he gets the idea, *then* you can climb off and go to driving him.

Teach the horse to perform while pulling the weight just the way he worked without it, with the additional performance of holding the rope taut when he stops. The rope should come straight back from the horn so that it follows the crease in his croup. (If he isn't carrying enough "weatherboarding" to have a crease, feed him more!)

With some horses it is helpful to attach an automobile tire to the chain on the log and tie the lariat to the tire. When the horse stops at your voice command, teach him to hold his position so that the tire is pulled out of its normal shape while he is standing. This will help him to learn to lean into the rope. Bear in mind that the tire should be used only when you are working at a walk, and it should be used only after the horse has learned to work quietly when dragging weight.

When the horse has learned to respond to your voice signals and will continue leaning into the weight on the rope when he stops, you may discard the off (right) rope line, coil the near (left) one up in your bridle hand, and mount. Now ask your horse to do everything you have taught him from the ground, making sure that he pulls straight and stands leaning into the weight when you dismount. Work him while you are standing in one stirrup. Have him continue at voice command while you dismount and walk back to the log. Then dismount and run a few feet ahead of him while he is walking. Stop, and when he has dragged the log up to you, put your foot on it and tell him "Whoa." If he does not respond, a jerk on the rope line coiled in your bridle hand will stop him, though the necessity for this is a sign that your previous training has been a little scanty.

When your horse will perform perfectly, regardless of whether you are sitting in the middle of him, hanging on to one side, or dismounted, you are ready to work him at a trot and lope. Two things must be continually emphasized—(1) pulling straight and (2) leaning into the weight when stopped. At this stage, take plenty of time to dismount, riding your near stirrup for a stride or two before you leave the horse. Let him move the log a few steps after you hit the ground so that he will not get the notion that dismounting is a signal to stop. It is a good idea to keep the longline in your hand for a few of these lessons just in case he forgets to stop when he should.

While he is stopped and leaning into the weight, put your foot on the log, move it a trifle, jiggle the taut rope, and then walk up the rope to the horse and pat him on the rump. Mount him and then walk him a step or two forward before you turn him to the right and release the rope pressure.

When you start roping, the horse will learn from experience that he should continue to the end of the rope and stop with his weight leaning into it. However, at least one roper of my acquaintance puts in an extra step of logging education just before actually roping. He gets a helper to attach a rope to the back end of the log. When my friend steps off, he allows his horse to take a stride or two and then has the helper put back pressure on the log. As soon as the back pressure is applied, my friend tells his own horse "Whoa." He gradually decreases the volume of the "whoa" until the horse is stopping and leaning into the rope when the back pull hits it.

My friend tells me that there are no shortcuts in logging for the man who wants the best in a heading horse, and the few phenomenal "naturals" that seem to have developed in spite of strongarm methods and some abuse are the exceptions that prove the rule. Even the best heading horse needs a refresher course in logging every few weeks, especially in some part of the performance in which he has become a little slack or sloppy. For example, if the horse tends to pull off to the side or to swing his hip away from the rope, a little driving work dragging the log by two ropes, one attached to each side of the breast collar, will straighten him out. If he slacks off on holding the rope taut, a little slow work with the rubber tire may be the remedy.

THE HEELING HORSE

The big job of the heeling horse is to put you where you want to be—when you want to be there. That includes, of course, keeping you there until you want to change position in relation to the steer. More than any other rope horse, the heeling horse needs training on being quiet and ready in the box, the kind of training I have detailed for the calf-roping horse. In team roping there are two horses in the box. Furthermore, the chances are that

Team ropers in the box. *Photo courtesy Louise L. Serpa, Tucson, Arizona*

a steer may cause more commotion in the box if he starts being contrary than will a smaller animal, and this will make more excitement in the chute to stir up the waiting horses in the box. The position for the heeling horse is in the far corner of the box, away from the chute and at the back.

He must be so trained that he will stand quietly but ready in that spot and let any number of cattle leave the chute; but when the right steer scores, he must be instantly at his place beside the header—just far enough away to allow room for the swinging rope and a nose or two behind. As the header makes his throw, the heeling horse follows the steer. When the header jerks his slack and turns left, turning the steer, the heeler also turns left *behind* the steer, so that his rider's loop, with the honda at the steer's hock or flank, will set a trap for those hind legs. If the heeling horse stops or slows too soon, he won't be close enough for the job. If he makes his turn too far forward, he will be going in toward the steer's head.

Some heelers want the horse to make a quarter-turn left over his hocks close to the steer just as it is turned completely to the left. Others want a horse to turn in a circle, so they can throw the trap just as the horse is crosswise of the steer. Some like to throw the heel loop when the horse is directly in line with and behind the steer. Wherever the heeler wants to be, the horse must have him there on time. The term "scotching" is used for the fault of the heeling horse that slackens speed too soon or stops too short. Such a horse causes the heeler's loop, of course, to fall short.

It takes time and skill to make the heeling horse that does his share of winning top money and to keep him at his peak of performance. Though he does not have to work on his own while his rider is dismounted, as does the header's horse, logging is an important part of his training and of the refresher course that must be given him frequently. He must unfailingly keep the proper tension on the rope when he is holding and must also release it and turn back on signal—without anticipating.

Some team ropers practice with a dummy calf, getting a little practice for themselves in setting the heel trap as well as school-ing the horse on being at the exact spot the roper prefers for heeling. They lope the horse up to the dummy, set the trap, and turn the horse to the left. Some say they can cure the horse that scotches by this method.

Team roper heeling at Chandler Rodeo. *Photo courtesy Louise L. Serpa, Tucson, Arizona*

"NO SON TODOS LOS MISMOS"

In no art or skill are the factors involved more variable than in roping. Many of the humans involved are of the dying breed of individualists engendered by the old West—anachronisms in this age of compulsory, standardizing education and computer programming. While there is much talk around the corrals of the excellence of Quarter Horses, a roll call of the mounts of winners at any big rodeo will include a motley crew, ranging from hot-tempered Thoroughbreds (many registered Quarter Horses show little but Thoroughbred blood on their pedigrees) to good old ranch horses carrying a drop or two of blood from Normandy or La Perche (with maybe a relative or two who look through a collar now and then back at the ranch).

Great rodeo performers, both human and equine, are individual and they are rare. Like great prizefighters and great opera stars, they come a very few to each generation. They cannot be cataloged, and generalizations about their training and their skills is self-defeating. Neither this book nor others of its ilk can map the road to stardom. They can, at best, suggest a middle-of-the-road course of action for the novice and then give such bits of individual wisdom as can be caught from the words or deeds of the great. Here are a few that I have gathered over the years. None is to be taken as a generalization and none has universal applicability.

GLEANINGS FROM THE GREAT

Start with the green horse and teach him first of all what a rope is. Time was when you'd rope a log, burro, or calf, step away, and let the horse fight it out. When you got the rope burns healed, if you ever did, you'd have a horse that watched a rope. Today we do it differently. We start riding the horse easy and carrying a rope. After a while we swing it a little or maybe gradually let it drag. Anyhow, we get him used to a rope without scaring him—so used to it that we can swing it under his tail, belly, feet, or anywhere without his paying any attention to it.

Next we teach a horse to follow a calf. Some will do it naturally; others take a lot of time. You can scare a colt off calves if you put him after one that scoots out in front of him with a lot of speed. Just take a young horse out where there is lots of room and now and then follow a calf or steer for a while, just to find out where it's going.

When you start to rope, get a narrow lane rigged up. You can use goats in such a place. Furthermore, it starts a young horse off working straight. Get your horse used to standing in the box while goats or calves are let out, plenty of them. Then rope one, or maybe just take the horse out quietly without swinging a rope at all.

Don't overwork a young horse. Many a horse starts scoring in the box because he's been made sour by overwork, and he dreads the pain of going after that calf or whatever it is. Also, he dreads the spur. Says one of the top rodeo contestants of 1967: "I don't want a horse trained to leave the box with a spur. Any horse will get away fast enough without a spur if he's handled right from the start."

The old-timers used to say, "One spur is all you need, because if one side of the horse goes, the other is bound to come along." But now we know that spurring on one side only affects a horse's balance, makes him want to lead with the opposite shoulder or crossfire, and so on. It takes some painful experience for a horse to learn to balance and lead properly for taking the jolt of a rope when he's being gigged like blazes in the left flank. (Ropers use only the left spur, because a spur on the right boot might catch on rigging and slow down dismounting.)

Another thing to watch with the green horse is your cinch. No horse can run his best if he's pulled in two by a cinch, and young horses, especially, are slowed down by a tight cinch. It ought to be just tight enough to keep a saddle on top, with the help of the breast collar.

Don't overcinch him, and don't overwork him. A couple of calves twice a week are enough for roping on the young horse, but ride him every day. When you haul him in your trailer, unload him every two hundred and fifty miles and let him get his legs to working normally. If you don't agree, try taking a ride yourself in that old rattletrap, standing perfectly still, mile after mile.

From the same star who warns about overcinching comes some excellent advice for the novice: The beginning roper on the young horse is a bad combination. The fellow who is in earnest about learning needs lots of practice, more practice than a young horse can stand without getting sour. The learner will do best to get a seasoned old campaigner, not too fast. He'll teach his rider a lot about calves—and horses; and he can take the practice—within reason.

From another star I gleaned a suggestion about teaching a horse to work a rope. Rope a calf by one hind leg. Even the tiniest calf will kick with one leg roped. That kicking will remind the horse of what he is to do. He'll keep backing to keep the rope taut, and he'll watch that rope.

The same star uses a railroad tie with blocks bolted to it at one end so that it is always propped up slightly. This he uses for practice roping with a young horse. With it he can teach a young horse to back straight as well as to know what to do when he backs into a fence. The same roper is also insistent upon not "grinding a horse into the ground on the first few calves he ropes." He keeps a light hold on the reins at the start of the run after a calf. He doesn't want the young horse to get into the habit of slacking off or "going down behind" until the horse sees the slack pitched up alongside his head. If the horse begins to slow too soon, he gives it slack on the reins. Then he keeps his weight in the saddle until the horse feels the jolt of the rope.

About bits, hackamores, and tiedowns there is no concensus among the stars. Their conflicting opinions would fill a book larger than this one. One of the minority who dislikes cable nose bands and short tiedowns says that he likes a tiedown, even on an experienced horse, but keeps it long enough so that it operates only if the horse forgets himself and gets his nose in the air.

The hackamore users are, very generally speaking, of two camps—the southern California boys who use a bosal that operates on the lower jaw, and the others who use the one of great thickness that operates on the nose. The latter variety is usually used with a fiador. Most of the hackamore users graduate the horse to a bit as soon as he begins to know what is wanted of him. Some, however, never come closer to a bit than a hackamore bit that includes no mouthpiece.

One trainer, whose rodeo career was nipped in the bud by a back injury, has started many horses that have gone on to big careers. He is at present somewhat tentatively using a bosal of his own invention, so far with marked success, in correcting high head carriage. It consists of a steel-rod frame shaped like a large rawhide bosal. On each side, where a mouthpiece might be attached, he has welded a three-inch loop that sticks outward. He covered the steel-rod "bosal" with braided rawhide but left the loops bare.

He fastens the rein on each side to the rigging ring of his saddle. Then it runs to the loop on the bosal, downward through the loop, and back to his bridle hand. I have watched this invention work wonders in correcting two young horses.

One never-ending subject of disagreement among professional ropers (and among polo players) is the question, "Should the horse know the game so well that he uses his own *judgment,* watches the cattle and the rope, and does what is necessary without bothering to pay much attention to his rider, or should he be responsive to his rider, regardless of what is going on around him?"

There are ardent advocates of each point of view, but some of our best rodeo performers say they want a little of both. I recently put this question to a friend whose judgment I greatly admire. He was never a big-time rodeo performer, but before he fell from grace and became a school administrator (would we could have more of his caliber in that work!), he was one of the best cowboys on one of the roughest ranges in Arizona, located in the Superstition Mountains.

A school administrator soon learns to avoid direct answers, and cowboys say as little as possible, so my friend ran true to form. Instead of answering my question, he told me a story. Here it is:

In the 1930's Pete Grub was just starting on his climb to international fame as a rodeo performer. He was entered in a steer-roping event in the Payson Rodeo. Steer "busting" was not prohibited in Arizona then. Payson, Arizona, put on about the wildest rodeo in the state. That was the year two of the boys put a rope around the neck of a visitor and threw the end of the rope over the oxbow in front of the old Oxbow Inn; just as they got the rope snugged onto a saddle horn, the sheriff came along and spoiled the fun. They did have one shooting, though, that year; but that's another story.

They had good, big, wild steers for the steer roping, and Pete drew one of the wildest. He was riding one of the best horses he ever owned, a big bay. Peter got to the steer right now, roped the horns, flipped the slack around the hindquarters, and threw the iron into the bay. That steer went high into the air and lit hard—but not hard enough. Just about the time Pete dismounted and started down the rope to tie him, the steer got to its feet and let out a beller. All Pete could do was wave a hand at his horse. That bay wheeled to the right, circling the steer, cutting between it and Pete. When he hit the end of the rope, he busted that steer hard. This time it was deflated long enough for Pete to get his piggin' string into action. Once, at least, it was a good thing that a horse acted on his own.

This story, by the way, is true, and is attested to by many witnesses still alive, including Pete, now a big rancher. The bay, if there is justice in heaven, is browsing knee-deep in celestial meadows.

10

CUTTING

No use of horses is increasing faster as a source of pleasure than is the sport of cutting cattle. Part-time ranchers, professional men (and women) young and old, are finding groups of horsemen active in the sport with degrees of skill comparable to their own. While everyone likes to be a winner, the desperate struggle to be a show-ring champion that infects so many areas of horse activity has not yet deadened the fun of the amateurs in the cutting arena. Of course, second-rate trainers abound to cater to the would-be champion owners who bring in a horse with the hope that in a few months (or even weeks!) the trainer will transform him into a champion cutting horse. With short iron pipes for beating heads into low carriage, sawed-off icepicks for gouging shoulders, tacks in boot toes for pricking elbows, and other gimmicks, the struggling trainer will produce in a short time an animal that will appear to the inexperienced and undiscerning eye to be performing like a cutting horse. The experienced eye immediately detects the signs of such phony training. The horse that has been punished on the bit will not drive out freely after a cow. If he has been jabbed and gouged for fancy side movements, he will be choppy and afraid to turn and move out when he should. Such a horse may display a lot of fancy footwork that will enthrall some spectators, but the knowing eye will detect his hesitation, his choppy movement, and his failure to get away from a cow and work her when the moment calls for such action.

Whether a horse is capable of being a good performer for a novice rider in little Sunday-afternoon friendly contests or a champion of champions, two things are absolutely essential for the development of his capability—time (at least a year of it) and plenty of good cattle. Of course, even with these essentials, a stupid trainer can ruin a good horse. He can work him too hard (more than a few minutes a couple of days a week at the start), fail to give him relaxing work outside the arena (with some "gymnastic" training thrown in in judicious doses), or fail to let him understand what is wanted. One of the most renowned cutting-horse men alive claims that to overdiscipline a horse leaves him with a scar that will never heal.

CHOOSING THE HORSE

Because training is a long and often costly process, it is wise to pick a horse that has the natural endowments of a cutting horse. On minute, specific details there is often violent disagreement among cutting-horse men. For example, considerable width between the forelegs is a *must* for some enthusiasts. Others say it makes for choppy movement. However, there is general agreement that a good cutting horse should be short-backed and stout-hipped; have his hind legs set under him; be naturally rather low-headed, with a neck of medium length; and by disposition be interested in play and learning. He must not be speed crazy, and he must be a handy mover. There used to be much talk about "cow sense," but most modern men in the know seem to feel that what makes a horse want to cut cattle is a fondness for play. The horse that will lower its head, shake it, and chase any chicken, goat, or dog that comes into his corral is pretty likely to be interested in working cattle.

From years of experience, I have come to have great respect for the old adage "No foot, no horse." My own first requirement for any horse on which I would be willing to spend money is that he have ample bone and feet big enough to carry him and do the work he is destined to do. Certainly I hate a big, "frying-pan" foot as intensely as anyone, but the foot that is shaped right can never be too big.

TRAINING

The general rule for the beginning age of training a cutting horse is three years. That is younger than Mr. Riddle allowed Man-o'-War to be campaigned; and the veterinarians tell us that some parts of the bone structure of a mature horse are cartilage until he is past five. However, five years seems too long for horsemen to wait nowadays.

In starting with such a young horse, care must be taken not to overwork him and to give him *very gradually* the gymnastic exercises that will develop his agility and his muscles. Such exercises are described in this book in the chapter on training the reining horse. They are the rollback, the pivot, and the spin. Any work that will help the young horse learn how to collect, "to get his hocks under him," is useful.

The cutting horse has to learn how to do three things—(1) separate an animal from a herd, (2) take it to a designated place, and (3) keep it from going back where it came from.

With a three-year-old, preferably one that is not too sensitive to reining (so he is not afraid a little later to work on his own initiative), the first lessons should be in following a cow. The best place for a youngster to learn this is on a working cattle ranch, where almost daily a green horse can be used at work that involves a little work on cattle. However, most modern owners of prospective cutting horses cannot give their colts such a perfect preliminary training. If you are one of such owners, your alternative is to start with a bunch of docile cattle in one end of an arena and show your horse how to separate an animal from the bunch and follow it for three or four rods up the arena. Use your reins to show the horse what is wanted, and take it slowly. Repeat the process with several individual cattle. If you have help, let a rider put the first cow out of the arena while you are going back for the second. Only a short time each day should be spent on these first lessons. They are simple. The horse has his attention on only one cow at a time and will soon catch on to the game and enjoy it if he has in him the making of a cutting horse (and you have the patience and intelligence to let him know what is wanted at each step of his training before you go further).

When the horse is adept and interested in cutting out a gentle cow and taking her out into the arena, he is ready to start toward the next step of his training—learning to head a cow.

If it is possible to pick a cow that will try to return to the bunch or one that wants to go on out of the arena in some other direction, you are fortunate. She will give the little practice needed at this stage without a turnback man. It is much easier for the horse to progress at this stage without the introduction of the new and complicating factor of the extra man and horse. Teach him to handle a cow by leading her just enough—not more than a foot or so—and to keep just the right distance from her. If you are lucky enough to have picked the right kind of a cow, you will have the opportunity of letting the horse stand and watch the cow for a few minutes now and then. It may be that you can put her in one spot in the arena and then move her into another. Whatever you do, it should not be long enough to tire the horse.

I once watched a pony loose on the range of the 88 Ranch near Superior, Arizona, when he came into the corrals for water. The trough was about one hundred feet long. The corral was a fairly large one with trough and gate at opposite ends, so it could be used as a trap. Button, the pony I was watching, had been used some for cutting cattle at shipping time but had never had the opportunity to develop his talents for competition.

On this occasion he found three or four cows in the corral when he came in. He carefully went to one end of the trough to get his drink. The cattle started to drift toward the gate as he drank. Suddenly he threw up his head, wheeled, and as the cows started to run toward the gate, he cut off one of them. He put her right back into a corner at one end of the trough, almost putting her into that low cement receptacle. For a minute or so he held her there, staying just far enough from her to block her every effort to join her friends who were heading out. Then Button backed off and let the cow head for the gate. Just as she gained speed at the prospect of wide-open space, he shot after her, turned her back, and put her in a different corner. From there he took her through a side gate that led into the remuda corral and found a corner there in which he seemed to think she looked pretty. Finally he worked her into the center of that remuda corral and then headed her straight for the lowest spot in the fence. Then he rushed at her, bit her spine just above the tail, and ran her into and over that fence! He came to a sliding stop just soon enough to keep from tangling his own feet in the wrecked fence.

Button is not the only ranch horse that learned to enjoy cutting, as tales around campfires disclose. I include this story of a little horse, caught as a suckling out of a wild bunch and raised as a leppy (orphan), to illustrate the spirit and interest that a horse will develop if given a chance, a spirit that must not be killed by overdiscipline or early overwork if the horse is to become a great cutting horse.

If you must use a turnback man when you start to teach your horse to head a cow, work with slow cattle at first, and take it easy. Teach him to work just ahead of the cow as you move toward one side of the arena, and head her before she reaches the side wall. As you work back and forth across the arena, the turnback man should not press hard and the cow should be a slow one. Daily lessons should be short. If the horse begins to lose interest, put him at some other easy work for a few days. Work him on cattle only a couple of times a week for a while. At the early stages of training, it is important never to work the horse too long on any one cow.

AIDS ON THE CUTTING HORSE

Even among the greats in the cutting-horse world, there is disagreement about the amount of control, or use of aids (hands, legs, body, voice, and artificial gimmicks), on a cutting horse. Most of them agree that no two horses require the same amount, and most of them agree that the use of gimmicks such as pins in boot toes, electric shocks in reins, and tacks in bridle crowns are taboo. The National Cutting Horse Association, Box 12155, Fort Worth, Texas 76116, and its affiliates throughout the country are doing everything possible to disqualify from competition horses showing evidence of abuse through the use of gimmicks. However, as long as owners demand impossible results from trainers, some trainers will turn out ninety-day wonders by the use of all sorts of gimmicks (often ruining what might have been great horses by making robots out of them).

I have been told by men whose judgment and veracity I respect that there are humans so endowed with an uncanny sense of what a cow will do and also so endowed with lightning-swift automatic reflexes that they can, with a touch of spur on the shoulder or flank, aid the great cutting horse in his job. I am still hoping to see evidence of such a performance. Certainly many a good man can speed up the performance of a sluggish or mediocre old horse by the use of spur, voice, or body balance. The only help of such nature I have ever witnessed on a great cutting horse was now and then on a hot afternoon at shipping time, when the great little bay Pima became a bit weary. His rider, Wayne Taylor, would give the little fellow a whack with the side of his boot on the shoulder to speed up a pivot. One such whack would usually be all that was needed to make Pima forget his weariness. Granting the possibility of the justification of extreme use of the aids by phenomenal horsemen on phenomenal horses, the novice (who will do well to get his early experience on a seasoned horse working slow cattle) should be very conservative in his use of them.

Generally speaking, the cutting horse responds to the aids as used on a good reining horse—or any other well-trained riding horse. The reins restrain. Used in conjunction with other aids, they signal balance. The legs (including heels and spurs, if used) provide impulsion and, in conjunction with reins, signal balance and collection. The legs or heels control the hindquarters. Any good horse has two ends, and the good rider rides both of them. Even a fair rider should be able to place a horse's hind foot as deftly as he would place his own. The horse responds to the signal of a leg or heel applied well behind the cinch by moving his hindquarters away from the side on which the signal is given. The cutting horse must perform with an extremely slack rein. (In the early public exhibitions, all reins were of braided white-cotton rope so the audience could see the horse was working on his own on perfectly slack reins.) Therefore the use of the leg or heel aid is usually extended on the cutting horse to replace the reins in giving direction, that is, the rider may use the right heel on the shoulder to turn the horse to the left, or the left heel to turn him right. While the use of a heel or spur on a shoulder never ceases to be a repulsive sight to me, I have seen the deft touch of a toe on a shoulder at just the right instant give a horse the added impetus he needed to turn a difficult cow.

Body balance is used by some riders as a signal—forward inclination signaling for speed, backward signaling stop or back up, leaning to the side signaling for a turn. Such signals can be a very bad thing, especially when used by the novice. They are like the use of the leg grip for signaling. What happens when the leg grip or a lean this way or that of the body is necessary to keep the rider in the saddle? In a sense, every move of every part of the rider's body is a signal for the well-trained horse with whom his rider has perfect rapport. However, the deliberate use of body signals can very easily be carried too far.

Horses ridden by men who use voice signals soon acquire quite a vocabulary of words that have meaning for them—even profane ones. Such a horse can understand commendation when he is doing well; a calm word will steady him and a sharp one rouse him. In the old days of the draft horse, it was fairly common to see a horse working without lines in timber or in a small garden with rows of tiny, delicate plants. By voice alone, he could be turned, started, stopped, held to such a careful snail's pace that one could scarcely see him move, or stopped with his weight in the collar to hold a log on the skids. We do not carry the voice signal that far with the horse under saddle, but recalling the draft horse points up the fact that the horse can respond to the human voice.

RIDING THE CUTTING HORSE

General rules for riding the cutting horse are similar to those for riding the reining horse. Keep body weight forward off the horse's loins, especially when stopping and starting. Every move of the rider's body should be an extension of the rhythmic movement of the horse. Keep your inner thighs deep in the saddle and keep the insides of your legs from knee to calf in contact with the horse. Keep heels down and ankles springy but not tense. Toes may be a trifle farther out than riding masters prescribe, but the rider whose toes point straight out will have daylight between his knees and the saddle. This may be fatal.

Some cutting-horse authorities recommend long stirrups to keep the rider deep in the saddle; others recommend short ones so that he can rise and use his ankles for springs if he fails to keep with the sudden movements of his horse. The middle ground is best. Use a medium stirrup leather so that the knee can be comfortably bent when the heels are down and feet directly under the body.

In riding a cutting horse, the right hand is on the saddle horn. It is permissible to grasp the horn, but much of the time the appropriate position is for the palm to be flat on top of the horn.

E. H. Mooer's Patty Conger in cutting-horse contest, Pinal County, Arizona. *Photo courtesy Louise L. Serpa, Tucson, Arizona*

Certainly quick forward movements can be prevented from putting the rider "behind the horse" by reliance on the horn. However, the rider whose body is thrown back, his head and shoulders directly over the horse's loins and his right arm stretched to its full length by the fist that clutches the horn, is handicapping his horse. The horn is merely an aid, not a hanging strap like those in the old streetcars.

Now that the five-gaited horse no longer does five gaits, it is my feeling that the skill of the good cutting-horse rider exceeds that of all other performers in our public equestrian displays. The good rider and the good horse perform like expert ballroom dancers. The most minute movement of either is reflected in the other. The dancer does not say to himself, "We shall now turn left, so I shall tap her on the left shoulder."

His partner does not think, "His left shoulder is lowering, so I must step backward with my right foot."

Each partner is so aware of the other's movements that his own follow as surely as does one foot follow the other in walking or running. So it is with the good cutting-horse rider. His horse's slightest movement is reflected in the rider's own body. If the rider fails for one instant to be *with* his horse in this manner, the horse is handicapped. Such riding cannot be taught. It must be learned. The best way to learn it is to ride, with respect and humility, a seasoned old cutting horse working fairly docile cattle. How long does it take? About as long as it would take to learn to play a Rachmaninoff concerto. Maybe a little longer, for there are perhaps more variables in the cutting corral than on the concert stage.

THE CONTEST

When horse and rider have learned to follow a cow, to separate her from a herd, to take her somewhere, and to hold her there (and have also learned all the gymnastic exercises described in this book for the reining horse), there is one more movement that should be mastered, one which enables the horse to trot just behind and slightly to one side of a cow and at the same time keep facing her. That is two-tracking. Any horse that has been taught to collect himself and to respond to the leg aids I have described in the discussion of the reining horse will quickly learn to two-track. With the one leg, the rider keeps the quarters to one side of the line of progress so that the tracks of the hind feet are beside those of the forefeet rather than directly in line with them. Obviously the teaching must start with a slow walk for very short distances and progress only as fast as the horse can pick up the skill comfortably. In a few weeks, at most, the horse that can side-pass, pivot, and rollback can learn to two-track at fair speed. When he has added this accomplishment to his repertoire, he is ready to try his skill in competition with his peers.

In a contest operating under the National Cutting Horse Association rules, a horse has two and one-half minutes to display his skill. Time starts when the horse's name is called (for it is the horse, not the rider, who is being judged), so no seconds should be lost getting to the herd. Some riders lope toward it, but they run the risk of stirring up the cattle and thereby losing points. If you are a novice, starting your first competitive cutting, jog briskly toward the herd with your eye on the cattle, slowing and easing into the herd without startling it. You may have time to work two, three, or even four head. On the first one, you will show your horse's ability to enter a herd and bring out an animal. If you ease in too slowly, you may waste all your time and never make a cut at all. On the other hand, if you are too eager, you may be guilty of "charging," and you may drive your animal too far out from the herd. If you do that, the two turnback men may have all the play, for if your critter gets far enough from the herd, it will probably want to keep on going. You must, however, take it far enough from the herd to give you room to work, because as you work back and forth you may find yourself "guarding the herd," the name for the fault of working with your back against the herd. Furthermore, with five horses and riders—the two turnback men, two holding the herd, and you—your cut will be crowded into a small area: not a very good place for your horse to display his skill.

If you have done as the experienced do and carefully watched the cattle before the contest, you have picked a cow that's lively but not too fast, and your horse now has a chance to show his skill at working cattle. He will stay far enough away from the cut (the animal he is working) to give himself room to turn, but never far enough to lose her or let her beat him to the side wall before he can cut her off. This is easy to say but takes skill to do, and your horse will be constantly varying the distance between himself and the cow: he will *rate* her. You will be lucky if when she breaks for the side wall she runs just fast enough so that your horse can two-track, keeping just barely ahead of her with his head turned toward her. This is good for two reasons. First, it keeps him collected, ready to pivot the instant she stops or turns; and second, it makes a good show while avoiding the artificial sidestepping of the showoffs. Of course, if the critter goes all out for the side, your horse must instantly run straight, for that is the way he'll have to travel if he turns her before she is stopped by the wall. There *are* moments when the horse shows his skill by standing at just the right distance from the cut to gauge which way to move toward her; but the horse's job is to maintain his dominance of the situation. It must be the horse that moves the cow, not the cow that moves the horse.

If the game is going nicely and the horse has had some chance to show his skill, don't press your luck until the cow reaches that pitch of tension that makes her bolt for the herd. Make your quit by checking your horse with the reins and putting one hand on his neck while you turn him away.

This time, when you bring out another cut, you may "peel it off" from the outside. You have already shown your horse's ability to go into a herd and bring an animal out without disturbing the herd, and you may need all the time you have left. Of course, if there is not an animal on the outside that seems to be suitable for your purpose, you may have to go in and get one. This time, since your horse seems to be in fine fettle, you may want to pick one that is a little faster, one that will give your horse a better chance to show his quickness and speed; but don't press your luck too far and lose five points by having a cow get away from you.

See that your horse faces the cow at all times, unless he has to run all out. Let him quarter by two-tracking if he wishes, but don't show off by making him side-pass or do fancy footwork. The horse under the second-rate trainer can do all that, for he is a robot doing what he is told. Your horse is working a cow, and your job is to help him, not make him do tricks.

You may have time for another cut or two or you may not before the whistle blows and you hear, "Time's up. Thank you, Joe Doaks and Reed McCue."

Since this is your first experience, you don't expect a winning score, but if you have not fouled up your horse more than a time or two in that two and one-half minutes and you have no self-criticism for having overdone his warming up or having made some similar mistake, you are to be congratulated; and now you have the fever for which there is no cure. You have started on a road to which there is no end and no limit of enjoyment.

11

BARREL RACING

Barrel racing is a new sport, scarcely more than two decades old. It started in Texas, which abounds in good horses, pretty girls that can ride them, and fifty-gallon oil drums (the barrels). It was probably inevitable that these items should organize. The pattern of the barrels has varied considerably and may change in the future. The number of barrels has ranged from two to four. They have been arranged in a straight line, a square, and a triangle of varying proportions. Today the number of barrels is three and the pattern is that of an almost equilateral triangle. The size of the triangle varies some with the size of the arena, but the GRA (Girls' Rodeo Association) recommends one in which the two barrels equidistant from the starting line (twenty yards) are thirty yards apart, and the third barrel is thirty-five yards from each of the others. The contestant may choose to go either direction of the pattern, but most seem to prefer starting with the right barrel. It must be circled to the right, and the other two to the left. A flagman signals the start and finish of each contestant. Knocking over a barrel (even if it flips completely over and rights itself bottom-side-up) disqualifies a contestant, as does failure to follow the pattern completely.

Just as the dancer's foot moves as readily in response to her partner's volition as it does to her own will, so does the perfectly trained horse's foot (or any other part of his anatomy) move in response to his rider's volition. Certainly such a horse would be the ideal prospect to train for barrel racing. Such a horse should be the result of the training I have outlined in the chapter devoted to the reining horse. His quick response to the aids would let the rider hurl him toward the first barrel farther and faster at the first stride than any other horse. It would also enable the rider to leave each barrel in a similar manner—and leaving the barrel is even more important than turning it. The horse's good mouth would enable the rider to check him or rate him from a dead run at just the right moment and with perfect balance. His perfect

Barrel racer Carolyn Gould at Prescott Rodeo. *Photo courtesy Ben Allen, Rodeo Photos, Pasadena, California*

rein would enable the horse to respond to any signal of direction without yawing his head to the side opposite the direction of the turn. His skill at changing and holding leads would enable the horse to make the flying change of leads and to make the final dash for the finish line without swapping leads or baubling in any other way. Such a horse would need neither a bat (which some barrel horses so anticipate that they sour on their work) nor a tiedown (always needed on a horse that must be checked or rated by pain).

Although beginning the making of a barrel horse with such ideal material is desirable, it is rarely possible. Therefore, I shall devote this discussion to such compromise methods of training as are most popular today and most appropriate for the demand of speed in training.

Pick a horse with good feet and legs, a good middle (plenty of heart girth), strong quarters, and a neck long enough and fine enough to flex for balance. The barrel horse has to do more shifting of balance from one extreme (all on the forehand for running) to another (all on the haunches for turning) than does any other horse except the polo pony. You will want a horse at

Barrel horse and rider doing the impossible—making good time in mud at Intercollegiate Rodeo, Scottsdale, Arizona. Note rider's forward balance and light hand on rein.

least three years old and one with a level head and kind disposition.

If the horse you pick is unbroken, follow the directions I have given earlier for the first saddling and riding. Then follow as far as possible the program of training for the reining horse.

Usually the barrel-horse enthusiast will not take the time to put the fine rein and mouth on a horse I have recommended for the reining horse. A shorter method is to make the shift from the hackamore or snaffle on the completely green horse to a gag bit as

A type of gag bit now in high favor with some leading barrel racers as a training bit.

soon as the horse is accustomed to carrying a rider and making some response to the reins. The gag bit can be an ordinary snaffle, a double-jointed snaffle, a twisted-wire bit, or a double twisted-wire bit. The first two are available at most good saddle shops, especially made as gags. The sidepieces, instead of being rings or eggbutts like those of the ordinary snaffle, are semicircles or crescents. Each end of the crescent terminates in a little ring just large enough to permit a round leather strap, stitched like a round leather headstall or rein, to slide freely through it. This round leather strap goes over the horse's head. On the better ones there is provision for fastening the round strap to the center of the crownpiece of the bridle. The ends of the round leather run freely through the sidepieces of the bit on either side and terminate in rings for attaching the bridle reins. It is, of course, possible to make a gag bit out of any snaffle by using an ordinary strap

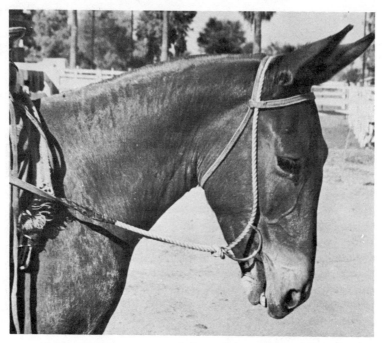

Similar gag bit, very successfully used in training saddle mule.

Variant of the draw rein. This is an improvement of the rigging used so successfully by the late Jim Faggin, manager of the Hearst Sonocol Ranch. Like Faggin's rigging, this one fastens to the center of the cinch. Then it runs through pulleys attached to bit rings and snaps into a D on the bridle rein. When properly adjusted, the draw rein operates only when horse's head is too high.

(preferably one not made of latigo or any other soft leather that will not slide easily through the rings). A piece of hard-laid rope makes a good gag if you are adept at splicing a ring into each end for the attachment of reins—an ordinary knot is too cumbersome and heavy. The homemade gag *must* be fastened to the center of the crownpiece of the bridle, because a side pull will draw one of the rings for the reins up through the bit ring. The factory-made gag bit's rings are too small for the end rings of the gag strap to pass through. For most green horses the double-jointed snaffle is best, though the difference between its action and that

Detail of the draw rein.

of the ordinary snaffle mouthpiece is almost negligible. The twisted-wire bit is, of course, more severe than the snaffle, and the double twisted-wire bit is extremely severe as a gag and will quickly make the corners of the mouth very sore. It is sometimes useful for a short refresher course or as a corrective on a spoiled horse.

A few trainers like to use a draw rein instead of a gag bit, but I feel that the draw rein severely limits the range of use of the hands. The draw rein is sometimes useful as a corrective for the horse that tends to work with his nose poked forward, so I describe it here. On each side, the rein is fastened to the front rigging ring. From there it runs forward, through the bit ring, and then back to the hand of the rider. The reins should be of leather stiff enough to run freely through the bit rings. Latigo or other soft leather or braided leather will not release through the rings fast enough when pressure is decreased.

TIEDOWNS

Though most barrel-horse riders and trainers use a tiedown regardless of what bit is in the horse's mouth, a horse will keep his head down with a draw rein without a tiedown. However, the gag bit exerts its pressure on the corners of the mouth, upward toward the horse's ears, so it can never be used satisfactorily without a tiedown. The most popular nose band for use with a tiedown and a gag bit is a large metal one or a cable. Such a nose band must be adjusted so that it rides on the nose about midway between the nostrils and the eyes. A low metal or cable nose band, a tight tiedown, and a gag bit are a good recipe for serious trouble. Any horse with spirit will fight desperately if his wind is cut off and the soft part of his nose tortured by such a combination.

Head chains are an alternative for nose bands. The nose may become so sore, even if the metal tiedown is replaced by a rawhide one, that the horse will fight it or will "pull his punches" because of it or will develop some other objectionable defense. In such a case the tiedown can be attached to a chain.

There are three ways in which the chain is rigged on the head, and there are ardent advocates for each method. In each of them, the chain is long enough so that when the horse is at rest there are six to ten inches of slack at the throttle where the tiedown attaches to the chain. In one method the chain goes from the attachment of the tiedown, upward through side slits in a brow band, and across the head behind the ears. In another method the chain itself forms the brow band, and a strap going over the head behind the ears is attached to the chain on either side at the base of the ear. In still another method there is no strap or brow band involved; the chain itself divides at the base of the ear on each side, one part of the chain going over the head for a crownpiece just behind the ears and the other part of the divided chain serving as a brow band.

Obviously gag bits and the tiedowns and metal nose bands (or chains) that work in opposition to them—gags forcing the head upward and tiedowns holding it down—can be the source of much abuse. However, in deft hands they speed up the work of training a barrel horse. Jane Mayo, one of the most successful trainers and competitors, and a reliable authority in the field of barrel racing, writes that she likes to get a beginning horse's mouth a little sore at the corners. The word "little" is perhaps the most important in that statement. The beginning horse should be taught so gradually to start, stop, back, turn, check from high speed to collection for a turn, and do rollbacks and pivots that his mouth gets no more than a "little" sore at the corners.

From the first, the horse must be taught to "lead with his head," that is, he should not yaw his head to the side on a turn. The improperly handled green horse will yaw on the side toward which he is turning if he is turned by lateral pull—plowline. If neck-reined, he will yaw to the side opposite the one toward which he is turning. With the beginning horse, neck rein, lateral pull, and leg aid must all be brought into play to keep him following his head. The sooner you can get your beginning horse to the point where you are riding both ends of him (a matter discussed repeatedly in previous parts of this book), the better.

It is perhaps the importance of this business of keeping the horse leading with his head that is responsible for Miss Mayo's seeming contradiction when, in one part of her excellent *Barrel Racing*, she advocates keeping considerable pressure on the reins of the barrel horse and then, in another part of the book, stresses the importance of the light mouth and the horse's ability to work on a loose rein. Until the barrel horse's education is completed (if that stage is ever reached by any horse), you must keep him well in hand, especially when speed is involved, employing all the aids and both kinds of reining as the moment demands. When you can call your horse a well-trained barrel horse, then, and only then, will you be able to rate him, turn him, or do anything else with him on a light or loose rein. The "secret" of reaching this point is care in proceeding only as fast with the horse's training as he is able to go with understanding and willingness. Another factor, though certainly no secret to anyone who has read this far in this book, is refraining from ever sitting back on the reins with a dead pull. The most frantic horse can be checked from an all-out run by a rhythmic but rapid alternation of pressure from side to side on a gag bit opposed by a good tiedown and metal nose band.

THE TRAINING

In starting your horse to run barrels, the ideal place is open desert where there are no rocks or holes—and no fences close by. Grass is slippery. An early fall or sprain may have an effect on the horse that will be difficult or impossible to overcome. Keep his self-confidence high by never asking him to work beyond his ability or where he will hurt himself.

If no desert is handy, put your barrels in a big enough enclosure so that there are no fences to hinder or aid turning. *Walk* through the pattern of those barrels; then take a short ride and walk through the pattern when you return. For as many days or weeks as are needed, walk through the barrels casually until the horse will do the pattern automatically. Vary the distance between the barrels frequently—different shows have different-sized patterns.

When you are ready to trot around the barrels, head the horse at the spot beside each barrel where he will make tracks when he is alongside it. If a horse is running fast at a barrel and aiming straight at it, he has to make a slight but lightning-swift turn when he gets to it. For instance, if you are approaching the first barrel (assume it is the one on the right) straight on, you will have to turn slightly to the left when you reach it so that you can circle it to the right. Your horse will have to make either two fast changes of lead or one little left turn on a false lead to be in the right lead for turning the barrel.

As you trot the pattern, keep your horse in a straight line until his hip is beside the barrel. *Then* turn him. Use your left leg behind the cinch, if need be, to keep his quarters from flopping to the outside of the turn when you make a right turn (the opposite for a left). Your turn around each barrel should end as the horse is headed straight for the next barrel. This will get him a square start when leaving each barrel. A twisting start has lost many a race.

When you are ready to start galloping around the barrels, watch those quarters again. Keep them in. Centrifugal force seems to make them flop out at the turns, but I suspect that sometimes a horse is driving his forefeet into the ground pretty hard and the sliding hind feet have no place to go but out. If so, you must collect him a little more as you get to each barrel. Be sure you do all your checking and collecting *before* you start to turn. Keep a straight line until that hip is beside the barrel and that inside forefoot is ready to come up, squeeze his hocks under him, and lift him around that barrel—not too close; three or four strides ought to get him nicely around to the point at which he is squarely facing the next barrel. Be sure he is facing it squarely; then jump him out by a quick release of rein and a squeeze with the heels (while you are as far forward as you can squeeze in a stock saddle).

Some horses need the help of a bat to get them away from each barrel, and some need a spur behind the cinch to help them bend their bodies around each barrel (to the rider it seems as though the good horse is bending his body around the rider's inside leg). However, the less bat and spur you have to use, the better your horse and the better your chance of winning. Furthermore, what horse likes to embark on a venture which he has learned from experience will bring inevitably the gouge of a spur and the sting of a bat? I'm sure that if horses could talk, we'd learn that it is the horse that *wants* to win, the one with his heart in his work, that brings in the prize money most of the time.

If your first barrel on a race is the right one, you have one important job to do between the time your horse leaves it and the time you have to help him check and collect himself for the next turn. That job is to help him execute a flying change of leads. He has gone around that first barrel on a right lead. Maybe, if you got your weight off his left shoulder soon enough and he drove hard enough on that first stride of leaving the barrel, he changed to the left lead as he left the first barrel. If so, your job is done. However, if he is on the right when he heads out toward the second barrel, get your weight over his right shoulder (contrary to the practice of the high-tail showmen) and help him with a little leg aid on the right if necessary. If your horse is a little green and a bit slow on the change or tends to change in front without changing behind, hang on to the horn and lean out to the right to get that left lead. Use your right leg well behind the cinch to give him a little burst of speed. That will make almost any horse shift from right to left. If you doubt this, take time out and go to any Monte Foreman Clinic, where all your doubts will be dispelled.

As you leave, turn the last barrel; remember that it has no roots in the ground. Don't be in such a hurry that you turn into it. When you leave it, your horse may be the kind that needs a reminder with the bat, but don't try to bat more speed out of him than God, and his sire and dam, put into him. Help him by being well forward in your saddle as he leaves the barrel. That horn on *your* saddle isn't just to tie a calf to. Use it! It may help get your weight where it belongs. You're in a barrel race, not an equitation class. It's the horse that counts, not your pride.

No matter how well your horse is trained or how well nature has endowed him with the qualities of a good barrel horse, if you are not "with him" at every move of every muscle, he cannot win. To help him, ride a balanced seat, but be ready to be farther forward than that at the instant he throws his balance forward to leave a barrel. Don't be afraid to use your saddle horn to help you get forward or to get your weight (small though it may be) off the shoulder the horse is starting to lead with.

Ride down on the inside of your thighs and with the inside of your legs from thigh to upper calf snugged in close to the saddle. If you are "with your horse" and your upper legs are where they belong, you don't have to worry about your feet. They can't help being right where they belong—right under your body weight, with toes just slightly out.

Your stirrups should be just long enough so you can stand in them, with your legs where they belong, and have about four or five inches of daylight between you and the seat of your saddle. The saddle to ride is the one you have become accustomed to and like to ride just for fun. And, by the way, don't forget to take that barrel horse out for a leisurely fun ride now and then. It will improve your riding, and it will be good for his nerves.

12

THE TRAIL HORSE

The label "trail horse" is a loose one. It is applied today to a horse that is used as a mount for the organized rides, such as the annual Twain-Harte Ride in the High Sierras, that are becoming popular from coast to coast. It is applied to the horse used for the competitive rides, such as the annual one-hundred-mile Tevis Cup Ride. In horse-show parlance, it is applied to the horse that competes in trail-horse classes.

In trail classes the horse is required to do various things that are supposed to indicate his suitability for trail use. The feats required in such classes may include going up a short ramp and into a box designed to resemble a trailer, going up to a gate and moving so that the rider can comfortably open and close it (in some instances an object that would ordinarily frighten a horse is placed close to the gate), and backing through a maze made of poles placed on short supports and just wide enough to permit a horse to back through them without knocking them down if he is extremely careful. Another common feat is the traversing of a seesaw, across which the horse must walk without becoming frightened and increasing speed when he reaches the center and the platform tips downward ahead of him.

There is also usually some obstacle the horse must traverse to test his ability to pick his footing carefully, such as a group of automobile tires he must walk across. One year the popular obstacle for this test was a half-dozen short lengths of telephone pole laid parallel just far enough apart to admit one hoof. This device lost its popularity because the poles rolled easily and injured some animals. Another feat occasionally used is a low jump, which the horse takes quietly while mounted. Then the rider dismounts and leads the horse across the jump. Before this obstacle was well enough known to be anticipated by contestants, many a gentle horse refused to be led across the three-foot barrier. New obstacles are continually being invented (though I should not be surprised to see horse-show associations put a stop to invention by standardizing trail-horse classes), which seems to me a good thing, because trainers cannot drill horses for specific feats and must have them so amenable to the aids and so calm and willing that they can perform any feat required, new or old.

TRAINING

The ideal training of the trail horse would include everything that is taught the reining horse except rollbacks, spins, and flying change of leads, though the ability to do these things would not detract from his value. However, the training of the trail horse *must* be done slowly. Each progressive step in the horse's training must be taken only when the horse knows what is wanted. As in training for any other purpose, there are times when the prospective trail horse must be reprimanded quickly, sharply, and with exact timing; but generally speaking, force and punishment must be kept to a minimum. Reining horses, roping horses, and others work at times under considerable tension. Extreme collection is a *must* at times. But the trail horse must be relaxed, calm, and willing, which he will not be if his training is hurried and painful. He must be more responsive to the leg aids (taught as explained in an earlier chapter) than any other type of Western horse. In opening a gate, for instance, he must respond to pressure of one leg, moving to either side, as in the side pass, discussed in the chapter on the reining horse; and he must also, when necessary, move sidewise and either forward or backward simultaneously. He must be able to pivot on his quarters and also on his forehand, keeping his forefeet in one spot while the hindquarters turn around it. The opening and closing of some gates require all these movements.

The trail horse must be taught to move forward unhesitatingly in any situation when given a slight signal by his rider's legs, but he must do so calmly and at the rate of speed indicated by the bridle hand. On the other hand, he must "take over" and calmly pick his own footing on a slack rein when necessary. Though that rein is slack, it indicates direction; and the horse must obey it, even though it seems silly to go through a mess of junk when horse sense could avoid the trouble by turning a few feet to one side.

Our mount must, of course, respond to a signal to stop; and he must also stand still while his rider dismounts and walks some distance, say, thirty feet, away from him. Then, on signal, he must walk immediately to his rider and, of course, stand quietly for mounting.

As stated earlier in this book, a horse should be taught to lead with its shoulder beside the handler—not lagging behind like a toy on a string. The trail horse should be taught to lead in this fashion, but he must also learn to stop on signal while his handler, at the end of the lead rope now, climbs over a two-foot obstacle. Then, on signal, the horse should hop over the obstacle. When he lands on the other side, he must not whip his hindquarters out in a semicircle around his handler. Instead, he must resume the proper position of a led horse so that he and his rider can continue for a few steps as if no jump had been made. Then he must stand while his handler mounts and becomes his rider once more.

BACKING

The trail horse must learn to respond to direction by leg aid while moving backward just as readily as he responds to direction by reins while moving forward. In backing, he must lead with his hindquarters, just as he leads with his nose when moving forward. The rails between which a horse must back in a trail class require right-angle turns. The execution of these turns without knocking down a rail is one of the most difficult feats in a trail class. It requires the combined effort of horse and rider. I have seen a well-trained horse slowly back through a maze and touch a pole as a right hind foot was being lifted from the ground. Instantly the foot became motionless as stone. At a leg signal too slight to be observed by onlookers, the horse moved the foot slightly forward and across in front of the left hind foot and onto the ground. Then the left hind foot shifted a trifle to the side and the right one again rose for a backward step, this time clear of the rail. That is what I mean by *combined effort*.

The construction of a horse's eye and its position in the head are such that without turning his head he has almost a complete circle of vision. The only exception is a space of a few feet directly behind him. This gives him better rear vision than his rider, for the rider has to turn his head first to one side, then to the other, to keep track of the rails through which the horse is backing. Therefore, if you are training your horse for competition in trail-horse classes, it behooves you to strain your intelligence to the utmost to communicate to the horse that he must watch those rails behind him. If he knocks down a rail, your first impulse may be to use whip or spur, or at least a loud-voiced protest. Any one of these will probably excite your horse, and excited is exactly what you don't want him to be. What you do to communicate to the horse that he should not knock down a rail will depend considerably on the temperament of the horse. Certainly, before you start work on backing, you had better establish complete rapport with that horse. Then by tone of voice (not volume) you may be able to communicate your displeasure to him. With some horses, being made to stand still while an assistant comes and sets up the rail again will do the trick. If for the first several days of work on backing you use only one pair of rails ten feet long, and you stroke the horse's neck and commend him each time he makes the backward trip successfully, he may begin to get the idea. Whatever you do, do not prolong the work at any one lesson beyond the horse's span of interest and attention. It is easy to sour a horse on this kind of unnatural work.

Not all the performance in a trail-horse class is of the unnatural sort. The contestants must do a good walk, jog, trot, and lope—all on a light rein (slack rein, if you will). The lope must be done on either lead. Occasionally a trail-horse judge asks for a figure eight at the lope, which means that the horse must change leads as he crosses the center of the ring. I have seen at least one judge ask the contestants to travel single file around the ring to see if each of the horses will maintain without fretting the space of one horse's length between himself and the horse ahead of him.

THE COMPETITIVE RIDE

We use the term "competitive ride" for the modern version of what was formerly called the "endurance ride." The earliest of these that I have learned of were European and were sponsored by men of the nobility or royalty. The horses were ridden to death, all except the winner; and even if he survived and lived any length of time after the event, he was unfit for work thereafter. Sometime after World War I, the United States cavalry instituted a six-hundred-mile endurance ride. The distance was covered in ten days. Rules were strict and somewhat complicated. Each day, sixty miles, no more, no less, had to be covered. Rations and condition of each horse were rigidly checked. Awards were made on the basis of points for condition at the end of the ride as well as for time.

Today's competitive rides are of similar pattern. On most of them a horse is penalized if he covers the allotted mileage too fast. Veterinarians stationed at checkpoints record the condition of the horses. There are regional competitive-trail-ride associations throughout the country, each with its somewhat complicated set of rules for classifying competitors and evaluating points. Many competitors make the circuit of their region each season, striving to be high-point winner, each in his particular class and possibly in all classes.

In addition to the regionally organized rides, there are also independent competitive rides. One of the most famous, the Tevis Cup Ride, is one hundred miles over rugged terrain. Even on this ride, however, riders must be humane. Several years ago a young woman made the trip on a little mare in sixteen hours, winning over a field of good horses. Ten days later the same pair won a seventy-eight-mile endurance ride, which points up the fact that today we do not ride our endurance horses to death.

CONDITIONING

There are several reasons for the difference between the old-time endurance ride that killed horses and the present-day ride. One of them is that today we know more about conditioning horses for strenuous work. I hasten to add that in comparison to what is unknown about horse nutrition (a most important part of conditioning), our existing knowledge is very small. Nevertheless, we have discarded many old wives' tales about feeding, care of feet and legs, and exercise; and we now know a little about the vitamin and mineral deficiencies of some of the diets horses have been subjected to, though in a very general way.

Charles Lakin, Arizona breeder of Quarter Horses and manufacturer of a very excellent and popular pelleted feed, was asked in a seminar on feeds about the value of additives in today's formulas.

"We are just beginning to find out some things," he replied. "So much is yet to be learned; but we just put in a broadshot of everything proved to be of value—trace minerals and vitamins—to make sure we have covered deficiencies."

Bulletins on the most recent findings about feeds and feeding are available from county agents, Four-H Club leaders, the United States Department of Agriculture, and all agriculture colleges. At least six months before entering a competitive ride of any sort, a horseman should make a thorough study of the feeds available in his locality and of their known deficiencies (they vary from area to area) and familiarize himself with what is known about the feed requirements of the horse.

One thing commonly overlooked may well be mentioned here. It is the "natural" feeding habits of the horse—so obvious as to escape attention. The feral (wild) horse eats at frequent intervals (if he can find forage). He does not eat much at any one time. Man confines him and thinks he is doing well if he feeds the horse twice daily. So remarkable a creature is the horse that he adapts and does very well on this "unnatural" routine. However, I am certain from my experience in putting emaciated animals into good condition and in keeping show horses in the peak of condition that the nearer we can come to the "natural" feeding habits of the horse, the greater the excellence of condition we can obtain. The total daily feed consumption can be decreased while the condition of the horse is improved if we feed at more frequent intervals throughout the twenty-four-hour day, giving appropriately small amounts at each feeding. Such feeding is, of course, impractical for the average horseman, but the man intent on capturing a coveted trophy is wise to consider what is "natural" for the horse. (Much nonsense is talked about what is "natural" for the horse. As soon as we put a fence around a horse, he is no longer in a natural condition.)

EXERCISE

At least six months before a horse is to compete in a competitive ride, conditioning should start. If the horse has had very light work, the amount should be increased gradually. Routine is as deadly to a horse as to a man—probably more so, for the horse is not subjected to the deadening influences of public schools, radios, newspapers, etc., that make humans docile and willing to accept routine. I was delighted to hear a feminine winner of a coveted competitive-ride award explode when a well-meaning spectator remarked, "I assume you gave the mare exactly the same amount of work *every* day."

After her explosion at the thought of such a horrible routine, the young lady very patiently explained that it takes plenty of wet saddle blankets to condition a competitive horse and that he must not stand idle for several days and then be ridden hard to make up for the rest; yet, she pointed out, he must have a varied diet of work over all different sorts of terrain. She also pointed out how important it is for the competitor to study the rules of the competition and be sure his horse is prepared for that particular ride. Within the past year or two a ride was won by an Indian riding an Arabian mare one hundred miles in considerably less than ten hours. (All contestants were rigidly inspected by veterinarians and had to complete that ride in good physical condition.) On that particular ride there was a gorge to be crossed by a rough trail that makes a steep descent of more than two miles and an ascent of the same length. The mare never broke her long trot as she was ridden down the trail. At the bottom of the trail her rider dismounted and led the mare at the same long trot up the ascent. Obviously the rider must have put himself as well as the mare in pretty good condition for that ride. However, the important lesson is that if the Indian had not known the rules of that ride and that they permitted leading the horse, he might not have had that mare trained so that she would readily lead at the trot up that rough trail.

The winning of a competitive ride calls for a good horse to start with, an intelligent and faithful human to put that horse in condition, and a good portion of luck.

POSTSCRIPT

Kipling said, "Oh, East is East and West is West, and never the twain shall meet/Till Earth and Sky stand presently at God's great Judgment Seat."

Though Mr. Kipling is a bit out of fashion presently among the more precious of our literary elite, those opening lines of *The Ballad of East and West* have an almost ominous relevance to the subject of this book. East and West are certainly coming closer together than ever before. However, they most certainly have not met.

The late Master of Foxhounds Henry Wynmalen said, "Complete harmony of horse and rider is the goal [of horsemanship]." Western horsemanship has a different goal, or at least it goes a bit further. Whether on the trail or in the cutting pen, a Western horse is expected to do a great deal "on his own." The rider's job is to avoid being a handicap. This demands skill in balance, hands, and timing. Many jobs the Western horse has to perform were unheard of in most parts of the world until very recently. Some of those jobs require equipment very different from the tack used in the East; and that tack—particularly saddles, because they put the rider a little farther away from the horse than do flat saddles of the East—requires special technique. A good horseman can "ride in both saddles," as the conquistadors boasted, but he does not confuse the two techniques.

Today Western horsemanship is growing in popularity faster than any kind of horsemanship has ever grown before. Just a few years ago Western saddles were never seen in show rings east of the Mississippi. Today Western classes are a popular attraction in shows in every state in the Union where horses are displayed. East and West may, after all, meet sooner than Mr. Kipling predicted.

NOTES ON EQUIPMENT

HALTERS—AND THEIR USE

The first equipment you will need for your new horse is a halter and rope. Until recently an unwritten law among horsemen required that a halter be supplied by the seller. "Sale halters" were available at every country store. They would serve to lead or tie up a reasonably gentle horse. Some sellers still abide by the custom and go even further than custom requires. They put a good Johnson rope halter on the horse as they present it to the buyer.

Halters of the type just referred to are the best for a beginning horseman (and many others) if they are of the proper size and properly adjusted. They are stronger than leather halters, regardless of the thickness of the leather, and they are cheaper. If a horse wears a halter when loose in a corral or stall, a new leather halter, unless well soaped or oiled, will chafe if it is not properly adjusted. However, there is one danger that is increased by the use of a rope halter in the corral: It will not break if the horse catches it on something. If what he catches it on is sufficiently solid, he may sustain serious injury as he struggles to free himself. Any horse, no matter how docile, will panic and struggle if his head is fastened so that it is pulled downward or so that he cannot move it in any direction. A leather halter will break if he struggles sufficiently. If the leather halter is a light one, the chances are pretty good that he will break it before he does any more damage than learning the vice of pulling back on a halter, a vice he is very likely to develop if he breaks a halter or two.

The Johnson-type halter comes in several sizes and should be ordered according to the approximate weight of the horse. It has two adjustments—one for the doubled rope that goes over the head and one for the length under the jaw between the nose band and throttle. If the former is too long, an itchy horse will rub the halter off over his ears; if the latter is too long, the halter will pull off under the horse's chin.

Johnson-type halters are now available in nylon in various attractive colors as well as white. Nylon is, of course, stronger than cotton, but nylon will slip in the metal clips that hold the parts of the halter together, as I learned the hard way when those pesky things first hit the market. That was in fly time where I lived; and a few minutes after I tied my horse with that brand-new fancy halter, a fly bit him on the shoulder. He swung his head to get at the fly, and as he hit the end of the halter shank, the nylon nose band jerked loose from the clip that held it. Fortunately, I was close to the horse and no serious harm resulted. I took the halter off, put the end of the nose band back in the clip, put the pesky clip on the plate of the trailer hitch on the back of my pickup, and hit it a couple of good swats with a hammer, closing it tightly on the nylon. I did the same with the other two clips. I'm still using that pretty piece of equipment (two-toned—very fancy!) now and then when I tie my horse where I have an eye on him; and I've had no trouble since wielding a hammer on those clips. (Mr. Johnson guarantees his halters, but I doubt that he would pay for an injured horse.)

This digression suggests a word of caution very important for the beginner. If a horse is tied by only a rope around his neck, he will most probably put his head to the ground if he is left for a few minutes. If while his head is down he takes a step backward to nibble a blade of grass or investigate an intriguing smell, the rope will move around on his neck until the part leading to the rail or hitch rack to which he is tied will pass between his ears instead of hanging down from his throttle as it did when he was first tied. When he raises his head, the rope will pull downward on the top of his head against the tender base of his ear. Panic results and havoc reigns. More than one horse, to my own knowledge, has met his death from just such a happening. True enough, many an old ranch horse can be tied this way with no trouble. Such horses are the survivors of much painful rough handling; but the valuable horse of today, one that has never been "choked down" in his youth and learned how to survive other uses of a rope, should never be tied with only a rope.

Similar disaster can occur when a horse is tied by the bridle reins. Let me illustrate. A valued friend of mine is a busy surgeon. His relaxation is riding with friends. He is an excellent horseman and good-naturedly enjoys an opportunity of putting me in the wrong on some matter of horsemanship. Finding daylight hours too busy to permit recreation, he now and then invites a small group of friends to gather at his suburban home on a moonlit evening and ride in the mountains in which his home is located. Because some of the guests are not horsemen of much experience and because the liquid refreshment enjoyed may lessen caution on rough terrain, the doctor puts a stipulation on all invitations: "No studs, no mares."

Because of that stipulation, I rode the only gelding in my corral on one of those delightful occasions. The gelding, Shorty, is a great old horse, broken in the old-time method, familiar with "what evil things the heart of man can dream and, dreaming, do." Before he came into my hands he had been used for roping, for bulldogging, for lion and bear hunting, and for anything else a Western horse can do in the range country. He will hop into a trailer like a puppy dog and stand tied with a shoestring.

On the evening I am recalling, coffee and doughnuts were served on the patio when we all returned from our ride, to fortify us for loading our mounts in trailers and wending our various ways home.

I had tied Shorty—good old, trustworthy Shorty—by the bridle reins to a hitch rail within plain sight of the patio and sat enjoying my coffee when a friend queried, "What's that loose horse eating at the hay pile over yonder?"

I glanced up, my eye casually taking in the hitch rail where Shorty *had been*. The animal enjoying the doctor's good alfalfa was Shorty, with nary a rein to his bridle! Obviously, itchy from dried sweat (the ride had been rather strenuous and we had cooled off the horses coming down the last mountain slope), Shorty had rubbed his head on the rail, got the bridle reins between his ears, raised his head, felt the downward pull, and momentarily panicked. Fortunately, the reins were very light, so they broke before he hurt his mouth severely.

When the laughter at my expense died down, the doctor gave me a lecture on the evil of tying a horse with both reins: "You must always tie a horse with one rein only, so that if it breaks, you still have a rein left to ride him with."

He did not have to point out that I, who have continually warned against the evil of tying a horse by the bridle reins, was afoot because I had committed that sin. Furthermore, I know an itchy horse will rub, and if tied where he can poke his head forward and down (to rub the top of his neck or head), he is likely to get it under whatever he is tied with, so it will pull downward between his ears when he raises his head.

Rather than detail gruesome casualties I have witnessed resulting from improper tying of horses—with halters and without— here is one of the exceptions that clinch the rule, which illustrates the rule that the Lord looks after fools, drunks, and the very young.

Against my advice, which on this rare occasion proved to be wrong, the Montana ranch on which I had charge of the horse operations had sold a three-year-old mare (one not quite good enough to become show material) to the banker in a nearby village for his little daughter to ride. Shortly after that transaction, I drove into the village to mail a letter. As I stopped at the post office I saw that filly coming down the gravel crossroad with two little girls on her back and one riding a bicycle beside her. The mare was walking, and the cycler wove from side to side of the road to keep her speed down so she could join in the chatter. When they reached the bank, which is across the main road from the post office, the riders dismounted. The cycler propped her vehicle against a telephone pole and the horsewoman, presumably the owner of the filly, tied her mount to that same pole by the bridle reins. Evidently she had received some instruction about tying a horse, for she tied the mare at proper height, which forced her to reach upward to tie the knot. However, she tied the mare far too long—the reins were long, and she used the ends.

I waited and watched for the trouble I was sure would follow. Almost sooner than the young ladies had turned the corner around the bank and disappeared into the drugstore (soda-fountain equipped) just beyond it, the mare moved slightly to dislodge a fly. In doing so, she touched the bicycle. It fell over, partially under her feet. She cocked a curious ear and put her nose down to smell the contraption. The reins slipped down on the telephone pole.

"Ah," I thought to myself, "as soon as that filly raises her head, she will snap those reins. She'll go back to the stable and do more than I can to educate her owners thereby."

But no, that mare merely stood when she raised her head. Fortunately, those reins were extremely long, though not so long that she put her foot over them as she stamped at flies. They were long enough to permit her to hold her head in a natural position.

In due course, the young ladies returned to their means of transportation. Without bothering to untie the filly, they turned their attention immediately to the bicycle. That being placed upright in the hands of its owner, the remaining two started, with mutual assistance, to clamber up on the filly, but stopped when one of them remembered that the animal was still tied. That condition remedied, they mounted and rode off, leaving me standing shaking my head and thinking what a wonderful creature the horse is, especially one of the breed of that registered three-year-old.

After recalling that incident, it is with some hesitancy that I assert that any horseman who has any intention of tying his horse should carry with him at all times a rope halter or light leather halter and a good halter shank (half-inch stout rope or leather). If he uses a bridle equipped with a stout nose band, he may carry only a good half-inch cotton rope long enough (nine or ten feet) to go around the horse's neck (where it is to be tied with a bowline or other knot that will not slip and allow the rope to choke the horse) and pass it through the lower part of the nose band. Passing the rope through the nose band will prevent it from slipping around and getting over the top of the horse's head. If such a method of tying is used, the reins must be gathered up and knotted around the cheekpiece and brow band of the bridle so that they will not get under the horse's feet or back over the

196 Notes on Equipment

saddle horn, where they will possibly make the horse pull back if one of them happens to become caught under the end of the hitch rail or in a branch of a tree. Also, when tying a horse in such a manner, it is wise to tighten the throatlatch a hole or two so that the horse cannot rub his bridle off. (A throatlatch should always be loose enough when riding to allow for the increase in circumference of the neck when a horse flexes at the poll. This means that four fingers of the hand can be inserted under it comfortably when the horse is at rest.)

BRIDLES

The function of a bridle is to keep the bit from falling out of a horse's mouth. The simplest form of one is a strap that fastens to one ring at the top of one side of the bit, goes over the horse's head just behind the ears, and thence down to the ring at the top of the other side of the bit. This strap has a foot-long slit in it, starting about fourteen inches above the right bit ring. The horse's right ear sticks through the slit. If there were no slit with an ear poked through it, the strap over the head would work backward on the horse's neck when he moves, raises his head, and bends his neck at the poll. Then, when he straightened his neck, the strap would be so tight that it would pull the bit up uncomfortably in the corners of his mouth. In other words, the slit is necessary to keep the bridle in place at the top of the head. If the slit is too short or in the wrong place or made of stiff, heavy, new leather, it will chafe the base of the right ear. Also, if the bridle is stiff, the bit heavy, and the horse a head-tosser, the bridle can be tossed off over the horse's ears.

I like a split ear bridle and use no other kind. It is simple and light. (Why load a horse's head?) My favorite horse has a head of surpassing beauty, diamond-shaped, with his large eyes set low. I don't want to break up the lines of the beautiful forehead with unnecessary straps or cover more of it than I have to. The bridle I like is of half-inch leather and has an adjustment for length on either side, so I can keep the slit where the ear will come up through it midway with no danger of chafing. Before I started to use my bridle, I tossed it into a can of neatsfoot oil. Then I wiped off all the oil I could, got some more of the surface

oil off by using saddle soap, dried it off with a clean rag, and let
it dry in the shade for a day before I used it.

There you have one finicky horseman's notion about a bridle.
Notions about what is the "right" kind of bridle are as numerous
as those about the "right" kind of horse, or even more so. Some
horsemen like fancy brow bands. Were I forced to use a bridle
with a brow band, I'd want one with as small and inconspicuous
a one as possible. Of course, if my horse had a long, coarse nose
and not much forehead, I'd probably want a fancy brow band so
that my mount would appear to have something between eyes
and poll. A fancy nose band might also cover up some of the
nose.

When a horse starts to sweat, he will rub his head if he has any
opportunity to do so. The more straps, loops, buckles, and billets
there are on the bridle, the greater the damage a good rub will do
and the more difficult will be any repair on the bridle. Stiff, heavy
leather is more likely to chafe the skin of a horse's head than soft
leather. Some varieties of soft leather stretch. This, however, does
no harm if the owner watches and adjusts the bridle to compensate for the stretch. The only real nuisance in the stretch of
leather occurs in a chinstrap. A new chinstrap properly adjusted
will stretch as soon as it is wet, as it certainly will be from the
horse's saliva or sweat in due time. Then it will allow the shank of
the bit to come back so far that the curb loses its leverage. Worse
than that, with some bits the strap may press the corners of the
horse's mouth against the ends of the mouthpiece of the bit and
pinch them painfully. Many an old ranch horse has calluses at the
corners of his mouth to testify to this fact. The habit of head
tossing is often started by this pinching of the corners of the
mouth between a too loose chinstrap and the mouthpiece of the
bit. A curb chain used instead of a strap eliminates this trouble. A
word of caution here: There is a popular chain on the market
(popular because it requires no curb hooks, I suppose); this
chain attaches to the bit by soft, stretchy little leather straps at
either end that pinch! Such a curb chain must have been invented
by a man with a fiendish sense of humor.

Nylon bridles are finding some favor. If the diameter of the
nylon is large enough to preclude cutting into the skin, they are

probably satisfactory, though I suspect they are difficult to repair. The bridle made of layers of leather stitched together is also a nuisance to repair.

Adjustments for length of the headstall should be at the cheek, not at the top of the head. The kind of bridle with a headstall of a long strap doubled over the head is usually displayed with the adjustment buckle at the top of the head. This is easily shifted to the side. When so shifted, care must be taken to see that the buckle is at the end of the strap coming *up* from the bit on the left side (left is the side for any single adjustment), so the billet or tab end, the one with holes in it, will point downward and not be sticking upward to flop around or against the horse's eye when he moves. The same care should be taken with throatlatches. They must be put in the bridle so that the buckle end of the strap comes under the throttle and up to meet the tab end midway between brow band and throttle. Thus the tab end points downward. If it points upward, it flops in an irritating manner just below the horse's ear. Furthermore, it brands the owner as a greenhorn. In similar manner, the buckle and the nose band should come *up* from beneath the horse's jaw and the tab end should come from the front of the nose and point toward the jawbone. Nose bands, of course, buckle on the left side.

Cheekstraps should be adjusted so that the bit hangs snugly up in the corners of the mouth but without pulling or wrinkling them. Trainers sometimes drop the bit for special purposes, but leave that up to them. Trainers also sometimes use tight nose bands, but tight nose bands indicate a fault that must be corrected (or an ignorant and inhumane trainer). Of course, a loose and flopping nose band does not look trim, but the strap should be loose enough so that the horse can yawn without discomfort.

Choose whatever style of bridle suits your fancy, but keep it soft with saddle soap, have it properly adjusted, and have the billets all pointing in the right direction. Better watch that brow band, too, and see that it does not slip downward and tighten the throatlatch and rub an eye.

SADDLES

Early Western saddles were secured on the horse's back by two stout straps. One went over the front of the tree. It terminated at

each end in a big ring at the bottom of either side of the front of
the tree. The other strap went over the rear of the tree just
behind the cantle. It, too, terminated in big rings on either side at
the bottom of the tree. Those rings were just below the cantle. To

Double-rig saddle, as commonly used in many parts of the Southwest.
Note spacer between cinches.

those four rings—two on either end of the front strap and two on
either end of the rear strap—was given the name "rigging rings."
On the double-rigged, or full-rigged (both terms were used for
the same rigging), saddle, the front cinch was attached to the
forward rings by latigo straps; and the hind cinch was attached to
the rear rings (the cinches held the correct distance apart under
the horse's belly by a "spacer" strap).

In those areas of the West where a single cinch was preferred,
the straps over the front and rear of the tree terminated in one

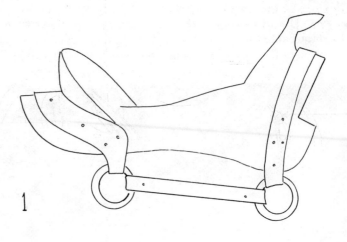

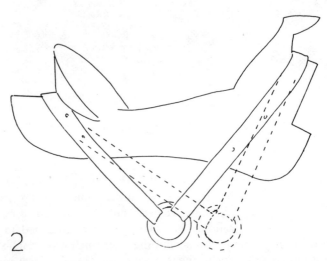

Double-rigged tree: 1. Stock saddle tree with full rigging. 2. Stock saddle tree with center-fire rigging (three-quarter rigging shown in dotted lines).

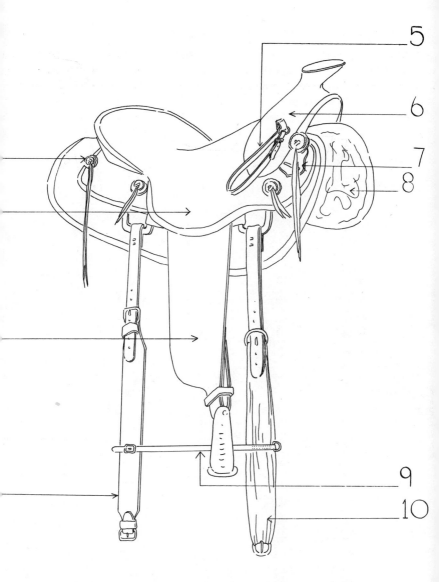

Stock saddle, off side: 1. Leather button (or metal conch). 2. Seat jockey. 3. Fender, or rosadero. 4. Hind cinch. 5. Rope strap. 6. Swell, fork or front. 7. Latigo carrier. 8. Sheepskin lining. 9. Cinch spacer. 10. Front cinch.

large ring on either side, both front and rear straps being attached to the same ring. When the rear strap was considerably longer than the front strap, allowing the ring on each side to be well forward, the saddle was said to have a three-quarter rig. If

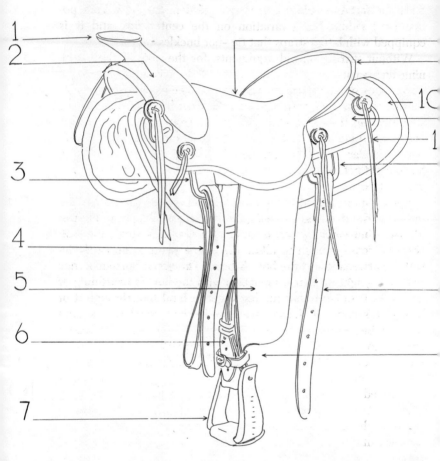

Stock saddle, near side: 1. Horn. 2. Fork. 3. Front-rigging ring. 4. Latigo. 5. Fender, or rosadero (made in one piece with stirrup leather on this saddle). 6. Stirrup leather. 7. Stirrup. 8. Seat. 9. Cantle. 10. Skirt. 11. Upperflank skirt. 12. String. 13. Hind-cinch ring. 14. Hind cinch. 15. Stirrup-leather buckle strap.

below the midpoint of the tree, the saddle was said to be a "center fire." The arguments about which type of rigging is best, even for specific purposes, have never been settled. Variations on those old riggings have been too numerous to detail here. The most comfortable saddle I have ever ridden, the New York policeman's saddle, has a variation on the center fire, and it is equipped with latigo straps that tie—not buckles.

Without stirring up old arguments, for the sake of the beginning horseman, let us consider some of the advantages and disadvantages of each type of rigging. On steep-shouldered horses that have arms (the bone between the most forward point of the shoulder and the elbow—the joint just in front of the cinch) that are almost parallel with the ground (good ones are more nearly perpendicular), a full-rigged saddle is very likely to chafe the horse right behind the elbow. This can easily cause an injury that is hard to cure.

For inexperienced horsemen, the double-rigged saddle has the very real disadvantage of being a dangerous contraption. First of all, the hind cinch, which is actually a two-inch strap, must always be loose enough to allow the whole hand to be easily inserted between it and the horse's belly. The green horseman may pull it too tight, so that it interferes with the horse's breathing; or he leaves it so loose that the horse gets a hind foot through it or brush gets under it. I have seen one serious accident resulting from an inexperienced horseman using a full rig with the spacer strap so long that the hind cinch got back into the horse's flank. A frequent accident is the tearing up of a saddle and ruining of a horse by undoing the front cinch first (before the hind one is unfastened) when taking a saddle off, or of fastening the hind cinch first when putting the saddle on. If a horse happens to move or shake himself when only a hind cinch is fastened, the saddle will move, tighten up that hind cinch, and make the horse panic.

The advantages of the full rig, amounting to absolute necessity in some kinds of work, are several. First of all, the double-rigged saddle will stay in place without having the cinches pulled uncomfortably tight. Most ropers consider the full rig a necessity, because when an animal is roped and the rider steps off his horse, the hind cinch prevents the saddle from tipping up on its front end. Steer ropers use a full-rigged saddle and add a breast strap to it. The center-fire saddle will slip backward on most horses in going up steep hills unless a breast strap is used. A horse used to a single cinch is likely to be frightened and become hysterical when a double cinch is put on him unless for the first few times the hind cinch is held within an inch or two of the front cinch under his belly by the spacer strap and is very loose. Of course, there is no problem in changing from a double to a single cinch.

The type of seat a saddle should have is a matter of even more controversy than the rigging. The early Western saddles had nothing between the tree and the man in the saddle except one layer of bullhide (with which the tree was covered) and a layer of saddle leather. More than ninety per cent of the Western saddles used by experienced riders today have built-up seats, and many of them have quilted seats of foam-rubber padding. The built-up seats slope from the front of the seat toward the base of the cantle. Monte Foreman, whose riding clinics are known from coast to coast, denounces built-up seats on the ground that they prevent the rider from getting his weight forward. Foreman also objects to the way stirrups are hung on most Western saddles and insists on having stirrups hung farther forward because it is difficult for a rider to get forward for rapid work if his stirrups are hung in the middle of the saddle, as is customary. Monte has marketed a saddle that bears his name and incorporates the features he advocates.

On the other hand, there are many expert Western horsemen who insist that because the cantle of the Western saddle is ahead of the rear of the tree, there is no danger that in ordinary riding the horseman will get too far back on his saddle. For fast work, they claim the built-up seat assists, giving the thighs a chance to carry the weight comfortably forward. I have heard little support for the swinging of the stirrups from the center of the saddle other than that it is the easiest and stoutest way to hang them.

Comfort

In all the controversy about built-up seats versus flat seats, and stirrups hung forward versus stirrups hung in the center of the saddle, to say nothing about padded and quilted seats versus plain seats, one very important consideration of saddles is conspicuously absent from written and spoken discussion. That is the consideration of comfort for the beginning rider and the experienced rider who has ridden only English saddles. For such horsemen, the saddle with stirrups hung in the old-fashioned way, directly under the rider's crotch, is sheer torture on a ride of any length. The saddle without a built-up seat adds to the misery. Saddles with such stirrups and seats have convinced many riders that it is impossible to ride a Western saddle. Another cause of misery is the saddle that is wide through the front part of the seat. Width at this point is also an impediment to getting forward on the horse when necessary. Only an expert saddle maker can tell how narrow a saddle can be right behind the fork and still be strong enough to stand roping, but for comfort's sake it should be as narrow as possible without sacrifice of needed strength. I know of at least two saddle makers who make stout saddles with built-up, padded seats comfortably narrow in front and with forward-hung stirrups if the buyer asks for them.

The most recent innovation in seats finding some favor among veteran horsemen is the padded, quilted seat. Many horsemen object to them because they know that the closer the rider is to his horse, the better. However, on the long, slow ride the quilted, padded seat is a comfort; and I know cutting-horse riders who swear by such seats because they lessen the shock of the sudden stops in the arena. Perhaps a half-inch of foam rubber and a thin layer of leather do not separate horse and rider sufficiently to interfere with good riding.

Novel Saddles and Economy Saddles

Ever since Juan de Oñate established the first cattle ranch in the West in 1610, ranchers have been looking for stronger and lighter saddles. Saddle makers for two centuries have striven to combine lightness with strength. Within the past decade or two, the bullhide-covered hardwood tree, the unchallenged standard of strength for many years, has been challenged. Aluminum, fiberglass, and some other materials have been used and put on the market with startling claims for strength and lightness. It is too soon to say that they offer a real challenge, for ranchers are not eager to give them a trial. However, the makers of one aluminum tree claim they are willing to stand behind their saddle in any comparison with the standard tree. They also claim their tree fits a back better than the wood tree and that it will not warp.

The fiberglass saddles I have seen are certainly lightweight. They seem to have a comfortable seat, but they are provided with "widowmaker" stirrups—small wooden stirrups—and are without fenders. I would not want my foot to be caught in one of those stirrups if I tumbled off or my horse fell with me. However, this danger can be avoided if hoods are put on stirrups as described below in the discussion of stirrups. Because fiberglass saddles are light enough for a child to lift onto a horse's back and because they are low-priced—less than one-third the price of a conventional saddle—they are finding favor as children's saddles.

If I were looking for a low-priced light saddle for a beginner, a saddle not necessarily as stout as a roper's rig, I would consult the proprietor of a good riding stable or guest ranch. Such men always have on hand many light, comfortable saddles which they purchase for much less money than a saddle suitable for heavy work would cost. Some of them occasionally use Mexican saddles, but most of them use saddles manufactured especially for their purpose by reputable American saddleries. There are good saddles made in Mexico, but only the practiced eye can distinguish between the good ones and those that "have teeth" (which will injure a horse's back) and are otherwise undesirable. Sometimes an obliging guest-ranch operator who buys his saddles in wholesale lots will let a friend or guest have one at cost. Even if the saddle has had a season or two of use, it is a much better and safer buy than a novice would be likely to get if he shopped around for a cheap saddle at bargain counters.

Stirrups

From the simple iron ring seen in Montana to the oxbow of the Southwest, the variety of stirrup styles is almost infinite. Without entering into controversy on which stirrup is "the best," a few generalities can be made. A stirrup should be large enough, especially from top to bottom, to permit a boot to leave it easily in case of accident. It should be heavy enough to hang down as the boot leaves it. It should not be made of aluminum or other material that will bend and trap the boot if a horse falls on it.

Tapaderos—leather coverings or hoods—serve at least two purposes. They are a very necessary protection when riding in brush, and they are a safeguard against a boot hanging in a stirrup when an accident occurs.

New Inventions

The new role of the horse as plaything and back-yard pet has led to an urban horse-population explosion, particularly in the Southwest, where riding is a year-round activity. The majority of users of horses in this new role are youngsters. An aside worth making here is that a record kept one year by the Western Saddle Club of Phoenix, Arizona, showed that more than eighty per cent of youngsters participating in its activities were on the honor roll in school every month of the year, and therefore wise parents are encouraging the horse-population explosion.

This juvenile influence is felt in the saddle business and has affected styles in saddles. Many youngsters do not have the money to buy saddles of the kind ropers use. Most of them have no need for such saddles. In considerable numbers they have turned to the use of pads, some with stirrups and some without. The pad is a great improvement over bareback riding for the horse's sake as well as for the sake of the laundress of jeans. A horse ridden continually bareback by a youngster will develop bumps on the spine where the pinbones of the rider habitually press. These little bumps enlarge when a saddle is added to the gear.

However, useful as the pad may be, its use is attended by some danger, especially when stirrups are added to it. There is nothing to keep the pad from slipping sideways, and it certainly will slip when the horse turns sharply unless the rider is very skillful. The stirrups provided on pads are of the small, light, wooden variety. There are, of course, no fenders to keep the stirrups from flipping up and catching a foot if the rider slides off on a turn. The remedy for the danger of slipping of the pad is to put a breastplate on the horse and attach the pad to it. A cheap and even better safeguard that can be made with a couple of straps and rivets is a Y-shaped strap. The base of the Y can be attached to the bottom of the cinch, and the ends of the arms of the Y can be fastened securely to either side of the pad at the front, a few inches below the horse's backbone. The remedy for the danger of the stirrups is to cut hoods out of old boot tops and fasten a hood (tapadero) on each stirrup to prevent the foot from going through the stirrup farther than the ball. Heavier and larger stirrups than the ones supplied by the manufacturer are also a help.

Before we leave consideration of pads, there is one other attendant danger that should be mentioned. Bareback riding and the use of pads without stirrups may be good exercise in balance if the reins are not used as aids for keeping it. That is a big *if*. It is very difficult to keep a good mouth on a horse that is ridden bareback by a rider who hangs on by the reins. And it is impossible to develop good hands when one is using the reins for balance. I have, in past years, made pupils spend hours in the ring riding without stirrups, especially those whose balance was faulty. I was careful to see to it that they did not turn their toes out or maintain their seats by constant gripping with the legs, *and I took the reins off the bridles*. (The horses were schooled and were working in a ring where they would perform by voice command. Similar results could have been obtained by working in the open and having a companion lead the horse whose bridle was without reins.)

GLOSSARY

AMBLE. A broken or syncopated slow pace.

BARREL. The body of a horse between his hips and shoulders. Also a fifty-gallon metal drum used for marking the pattern of a barrel race.

BARREL RACE. A popular sport originating in Texas, now popular throughout the U.S., in which contestants run a pattern marked by barrels.

BARS. (1) The part of the mouth on which the bit rests, between the incisors and the molars. (2) A metal device to hold stirrup leathers to the saddle tree.

BAUBLING. Making a mistake or objecting to performance of a required act.

BILLET. The end of the strap.

BOSAL. Round nose band of braided rawhide.

BOW. To bow a tendon is to tear the lateral ligaments of the cannon bone.

BOWLINE KNOT. A special kind of square knot that will not slip or slide and that can usually be untied easily.

BOX. The pen beside the chute from which a calf or other bovine is released for roping. The roper or ropers must remain in the box until the instant specified by the rules governing the event in which they are competing.

BREAK IN TWO. Slang phrase for bucking.

BREASTPLATE. A harness attached to center of girth and encircling the horse's neck at its juncture with the shoulders.

BRIDA, A LA. Riding with long stirrups, "forked-radish" seat.

BRIDOON. A snaffle bit provided with very large rings at ends of mouthpiece.

BULLDOG. To throw a steer by leaping from the saddle, grasping the bovine's horns, and twisting its neck.

BUSTING. Slang for breaking (a horse).

CABALLERO. A horseman.

CANTER. A slow, stylized gallop in which the center of balance is farther to the rear than in the gallop, and the action is higher. The sequence of hoof impacts on the ground is the same as in the gallop.

CANNON BONE. A bone that supports the leg from the knee or the hock joint to the fetlock; the enlarged metacarpal or metatarsal of the third digit in the horse.

CANTLE. Rear of a saddle.

COLLECTION. Use of impulsion and restraint to bring in the horse's chin, his hind legs well under him, and his center of balance farther toward the rear than natural.

CORONA. A decorative wool saddle blanket usually used in Western parade riding.

CAVESSON. A type of nose band.

COW-HOCKED. Hocks closer together than stifles or pasterns.

CRICKET. A copper roller or other piece of copper in the port of a curb bit or spade bit.

CROUP. Top of the hips of a horse.

CROWN. The part of the bridle that lies on top of a horse's head behind his ears.

CURB BIT. Any bit that employs the mechanical principle of lever and fulcrum.

CUT. To separate a bovine from a herd and put it in a specified place.

DALLY. A turn of a rope around the saddle horn.

DISHING. Turning the forefeet inward as they are raised for each forward step.

DISUNITED. Term used to indicate a gallop or canter in which two feet on the same side (rather than the diagonal pair) strike the ground simultaneously. Such horrible performance is sometimes called galloping with one lead in front and another behind.

DRAW REIN. A rein fastened to the saddle rigging and running freely through snaffle-bit ring to the rider's hand.

DUMB JOCKEY. Harness consisting of surcingle, back strap, crupper, side reins, overcheck (usually), standing martingale, and some sort of projection rising above the top of the surcingle to which reins may be attached.

EGGBUTT. A kind of snaffle bit in which the juncture of mouthpiece and sidepiece has some resemblance to the shape of an egg for observers with vivid imaginations.

ELBOW. Joint of the foreleg where it joins the body.

ENDGATE. A slang expression for the cantle of an old-fashioned Western saddle.

EXTENDED BAR SADDLE. Sometimes called officers' saddle. The saddle tree extends several inches behind the cantle of the saddle, thus keeping the rider off the horse's loins.

FARRIER. A person who shoes horses as a profession.

FENDER. A piece of leather attached to stirrup leather to protect a rider's leg from contact with a sweaty horse.

FIADOR. A brow band and throatlatch, the latter constructed of cleverly knotted, doubled rope of small diameter, used with a bosal to prevent the latter from dropping or being pulled from beneath a horse's chin.

FIRED, OR PIN-FIRED. A white-hot needle is pushed into a horse's leg at close intervals on the theory that a "weak" or lame leg will thus be restored to usefulness.

FLAT SADDLE. An English-type saddle, including some distinctly American saddles such as the gaited show saddle and the Whitman. The saddle that jockeys use for racing is also a flat saddle.

FOREFOOTED. Horse being roped by the forefeet.

FORK. Part of a Western saddle to which the horn is attached.

FORWARD RIDING. Use of the forward seat and the schooling and control that go with it.

FORWARD SEAT. Posture on horseback in which the rider uses short stirrups, inclines his body forward, and sits farther forward on the horse than other riders.

FOUL ROPE. A rope tied around the horse's neck. The lariat is passed through it to keep the horse facing the calf when it is roped and the horseman is hog-tying it.

FROG (OF HOOF). The triangular-shaped, rubbery pad that is the back part of the bottom of a horse's hoof.

GAG REIN. A rein fastened at the top of a horse's bridle and running freely through snaffle-bit rings and thence to the rider's hand.

GAIT. (1) The relationship and sequence of hoofbeats. E.g., the trot, in which a diagonal pair of feet hit the ground together; and the pace, in which the two feet on the same side hit the ground together. (2) The way a horse moves his legs. E.g., a horse with proper, or "true," gait does not swing his feet out to the side but moves them straight back and forth.

GALLOP. A gait in which the sequence of hoof impacts on the ground is as follows: one hind foot; then the front foot on the same side simultaneously with the other hind foot; then the remaining front foot, which last is said to be the leading foot.

GIG. Punching a horse's sides with spurs.

GINETA, A LA. Riding with extremely short stirrups, a Moorish style.

GRAZING BIT. A curb bit with a low port and with short, curved shanks.

HACKAMORE. Gringo corruption of *jáquima,* used to designate a much wider range of headgear than its Spanish source.

HALTER. A device of leather or rope to put on a horse's head for the purpose of leading him or tying him to manger, hitch rack, or other stationary object.

HALTER RING. Large ring on a halter lying below the jaw and used to attach halter rope or shank for leading or tying.

HAMMER-HEADED. Having a Roman nose and eyes set too high in the head.

HAUTE ÉCOLE. Literally, "high school," but usually a term used to indicate a set of movements or tricks the horse performs while mounted, movements said to be stylized versions of those he executes when playing in the pasture.

HAZER. A mounted assistant in a rodeo arena. Among his many jobs is that of taking the rider off a bucking animal after he has ridden for the time required.

HEADING. A term used in team roping to designate the work done by the man who ropes the bovine's head.

HEADSTALL. Bridle minus bits. May be either half of a double bridle.

HEART. (1) Extremely courageous, ambitious, and fearless temperament. (2) The girth just behind the forelegs.

HEEL, HEELING, HEELER. Terms used in team roping to refer to what is happening at the back end of a bovine in the arena.

HIDALGO. Spanish word indicating a person of high birth.

HOBBIES. One of the earliest-known strains of English riding horses. They were small and easy-gaited.

HONDA. A loop at the end of a lariat, just large enough to permit passage of the rope out of which the lariat is made.

IMPULSION. Impetus to move forward. It may be intrinsic in the horse and is supplemented by the rider's use of leg, heel, spur, or whip.

INTERFERE. When moving at any gait, a horse may strike a foreleg with his opposite forefoot, or hind leg with opposite hind foot. Thus he is said to interfere.

JACKPOT ROPING. Usually calf roping for a prize consisting of a "pot" to which each contestant has contributed.

JÁQUIMA. Specially constructed rawhide nose band and headstall (latter may be of rawhide, leather, or horsehair).

JOG TROT. A very slow trot.

JOHNSON HALTER. A patented rope halter widely used, especially throughout the Southwest.

LATIGO STRAP. A strap on a stock saddle that fastens the cinch to the rigging ring.

LEAD. A horse is said to lead with the forefoot that has impact with the ground independent of the other feet.

LEAD CHANGE. Change of sequence of hoof impacts with the ground at a gallop or canter.

LOG. Training a roping horse by having him pull a log or railroad tie.

LONGLINE. Walking behind a horse and controlling him by a pair of lines long enough to enable the driver to stay out of range of hind hoofs.

LUNGE LINE (LONGE LINE). A thirty-foot line of rope (cotton, nylon, or other material) used to get a horse to perform in a circle around a trainer.

MARTINGALE. (1) Standing: a strap that is attached to the nose band at one end and to the cinch or girth at the other. (2) Running: a Y-shaped strap attached at one end to the girth, the other ending in two rings through which the reins pass.

NEAR SIDE. The left side of a horse.

NECK-REIN. Use of pressure of rein on the side of a horse's neck to guide him.

NERVED. Having suffered a neurotomy, the severing or removal of a nerve in a horse's lame foot to eliminate pain.

OFFSET. A quarter-turn, a rolling turn with weight on haunches, using hind feet as a pivot.

OFF SIDE (OF HORSE OR GEAR). The right side of a horse.

OREJANO. A wild critter.

OVERCHECK. A piece of harness attaching to either side of a bit, running as a single strap up to the bridge of a horse's nose, between his eyes, over the crownpiece of the bridle, and thence to a hook or ring on top of surcingle or "saddle" of a driving harness.

OXBOW STIRRUP. Stirrup made of a piece of wood bent into a U shape and held together at the top of the U by a metal bolt.

PACE. A gait in which the two hoofs on the same side strike the ground simultaneously. It is, except when very slow, suitable only for harness racing and is the fastest gait a horse has other than a gallop. In many old writings the word "pace" is used to include all gaits other than a walk, trot, gallop, and canter. Many of the so-called Canadian pacers of colonial days probably racked or did a fast, running walk rather than what we call a pace.

PADDLING. Turning the hoof outward as it is raised to take a forward step.

PASTERN. The part of a horse's leg immediately above the hoof.

PELHAM. Curb bit.

PIGGING STRING. A piece of braided rope tucked under a contestant's belt or held in his teeth to be used to tie a bovine's feet together after it is roped.

PIVOT. Turning a horse's forequarters while keeping his hind feet in place. (Usually a 360-degree turn.)

PLOW-REIN. To guide a horse as a plow horse is guided; i.e., to pull back on the right rein for a right turn and back on the left rein for a left turn.

POLL. The top of a horse's head and the area just behind it.

POMMEL. The highest part of the front of a flat or English saddle.

PORT. The upward curve in the center of the mouthpiece of a curb bit.

POST. Rising out of the saddle on alternate hoofbeats of a trot.

QUARTER HORSE. A horse registered in the American Quarter Horse Register (sometimes euphemistically used to designate a horse thought to resemble registered ones).

QUARTER RINGS. The front rigging rings of a Western saddle.

RACK. A four-beat gait which may be said to be exactly midway between a trot and a pace. Each hoof has a separate impact and is followed by exactly the same interval, during which no foot is touching the ground. To the eye the gait looks more like a pace than a trot, but the ear can distinctly detect the syncopated rhythm that is counterfeit—a broken pace or a fast fox-trot, not a rack.

RAREY STRAP. A strap designed by John S. Rarey (a famous American horseman) to keep a horse's foreleg bent at the knee and pastern joint, used by Rarey in what he considered the main job of the horseman—getting the horse to understand what is wanted.

RATE. To rate a horse is to have him go at a designated or controlled rate of speed. In calf roping, the term is used to designate putting the rider in a position for roping and maintaining that position until the calf is roped, no matter how the calf dodges or changes speed.

REATA. A rawhide lasso.

REMUDA CORRAL. A corral in which are kept horses that are working on a roundup.

RO's. A very fine strain of Quarter Horse developed at the RO Ranch of the Green Cattle Company of Arizona and Mexico.

ROLLBACK. Stop, reverse, and change of lead from a full gallop.

ROMEL. A length of braided rawhide terminating in a single or double tapered strap and attached to the posterior extremity of closed, braided rawhide reins.

ROPER, LOW-DOWN. Western saddle with low cantle, very popular among professional calf ropers.

RUNNING HORSE. Thoroughbred, racehorse for racing under saddle.

SCORE. In team roping, the score is the distance from the barrier in front of the horse to the line the steer must cross before the barrier is released. In calf roping the score *may* be the same as in team roping; however, in some rodeos the horse's barrier is released the instant the calf is released, and in such events "score" means getting to a calf and putting the roper in proper position for the throw.

SCOTCH. A fault in performance of a rope horse caused by cruel, unnecessary use of reins in stopping. The horse anticipates the pain and stops before he is signaled to do so.

SCOUR. To have diarrhea.

SEAT. Posture of the rider on a horse.

SHANK. (1) Part of the curb bit at the side of the mouth. (2) A rope, strap, or chain, or combination of the latter two, attached to a halter to lead a horse.

SIDE-PASS. To move sideways, crossing leg in front the same as behind.

SLICKER. Raincoat made especially for riding.

SNAFFLE. A bit with a jointed mouthpiece.

SNUBBING HORSE. A horse from which a green animal is led.

SPADE. A Spanish bit, very severe and cruel in all but the most deft hands.

SPANISH BIT. Usually a decorated bit more severe than others.

SPIN. Turn on the hindquarters.

SPOON. A more or less spoon-shaped piece of metal on the mouthpiece of a spade bit, where the port is located in an ordinary curb bit.

STIFLES. Joint of the hind leg immediately behind the flank. The term is sometimes used to include the muscles immediately behind this joint.

STIRRUP LEATHERS. Straps that hold stirrups to the saddle.

SURCINGLE. The band around the body of a horse a few inches behind his shoulders.

TANBARK. The show ring.

TAPADEROS. Leather hoods over stirrups to protect feet from brush; also useful to keep feet from hanging in stirrups when rider falls from horse. They are frequently highly decorated.

TEAM ROPING. Roping done by two horsemen.

THEODORE. Gringo corruption of Spanish *fiador*. A throatlatch of light rope attached to rear of a bosal.

THROATLATCH. Strap passing under a horse's throat to keep the bridle from being rubbed or tossed off over his ears.

THROTTLE. The throat of a horse.

TIEDOWN. Any device connecting a nosepiece to a girth or cinch to keep a horse from raising his head extremely.

TREE. A foundation of a saddle. It is conventionally made of hard wood. Western saddle trees are covered with heavy rawhide before exterior leather, horn, and undercovering (usually sheepskin) are added.

TROT. Diagonal, two-beat gait in which off fore and near hind feet strike the ground at the same time and the near fore and the off hind feet strike the ground at the same time.

TRIP ROPE. Any rope attached to a latch on a gate (of chute, pen, or trap) for the purpose of remote control.

TURK'S-HEAD KNOT. A very complicated knot used for decoration or to prevent a rope from passing through a narrow opening.

TWITCH. A stout stick, such as a handle of a Boy Scout ax, with a loop of stout rope or light chain at one end. The loop may be put over a horse's upper lip and twisted tight to cause so much pain that the horse will be immobilized.

TWO-TRACK. Usually applied to the trot; however, a horse is said to two-track when he travels at any gait with his body oblique to his line of progress so that his forefeet make a track some distance away from the track of the hind feet.

VAQUERO. Cowboy.

WADDY. Slang for cowboy.

WALK. A four-beat gait with the same interval following each hoofbeat. In this gait there is no interval when all feet are off the ground.

WEAVING. The horse will stand in relatively the same spot for hours but will continuously shift weight from one foot to the other, as do some animals in cages.

WEYMOUTH. An English curb bit.

WHANG LEATHER. Very soft leather, usually used in strips for tying other pieces of leather together.

WING. To swing the feet out to the side as they move forward.

WITHERS. Highest point of a horse's back, just behind the juncture of neck and back.

YAW. When he yaws, a horse thrusts his head to the side (and sometimes in other directions) to protest against the misuse of the bit.

INDEX

Melvin Powers
SELF-IMPROVEMENT
LIBRARY

ASTROLOGY

__ASTROLOGY: A FASCINATING HISTORY P. Naylor	2.00
__ASTROLOGY: HOW TO CHART YOUR HOROSCOPE Max Heindel	2.00
__ASTROLOGY: YOUR PERSONAL SUN-SIGN GUIDE Beatrice Ryder	2.00
__ASTROLOGY FOR EVERYDAY LIVING Janet Harris	2.00
__ASTROLOGY MADE EASY Astarte	2.00
__ASTROLOGY MADE PRACTICAL Alexandra Kayhle	2.00
__ASTROLOGY, ROMANCE, YOU AND THE STARS Anthony Norvell	3.00
__MY WORLD OF ASTROLOGY Sydney Omarr	3.00
__THOUGHT DIAL Sydney Omarr	2.00
__ZODIAC REVEALED Rupert Gleadow	2.00

BRIDGE & POKER

__ADVANCED POKER STRATEGY & WINNING PLAY A. D. Livingston	2.00
__BRIDGE BIDDING MADE EASY Edwin Kantar	5.00
__BRIDGE CONVENTIONS Edwin Kantar	4.00
__COMPLETE DEFENSIVE BRIDGE PLAY Edwin B. Kantar	10.00
__HOW TO IMPROVE YOUR BRIDGE Alfred Sheinwold	2.00
__HOW TO WIN AT POKER Terence Reese & Anthony T. Watkins	2.00
__TEST YOUR BRIDGE PLAY Edwin B. Kantar	3.00

BUSINESS STUDY & REFERENCE

__CONVERSATION MADE EASY Elliot Russell	2.00
__EXAM SECRET Dennis B. Jackson	2.00
__FIX-IT BOOK Arthur Symons	2.00
__HOW TO BE A COMEDIAN FOR FUN & PROFIT King & Laufer	2.00
__HOW TO DEVELOP A BETTER SPEAKING VOICE M. Hellier	2.00
__HOW TO MAKE A FORTUNE IN REAL ESTATE Albert Winnikoff	3.00
__HOW TO MAKE MONEY IN REAL ESTATE Stanley L. McMichael	2.00
__INCREASE YOUR LEARNING POWER Geoffrey A. Dudley	2.00
__MAGIC OF NUMBERS Robert Tocquet	2.00
__PRACTICAL GUIDE TO BETTER CONCENTRATION Melvin Powers	2.00
__PRACTICAL GUIDE TO PUBLIC SPEAKING Maurice Forley	2.00
__7 DAYS TO FASTER READING William S. Schaill	2.00
__SONGWRITERS' RHYMING DICTIONARY Jane Shaw Whitfield	3.00
__SPELLING MADE EASY Lester D. Basch & Dr. Milton Finkelstein	2.00
__STUDENT'S GUIDE TO BETTER GRADES J. A. Rickard	2.00
__TEST YOURSELF — Find Your Hidden Talent Jack Shafer	2.00
__YOUR WILL & WHAT TO DO ABOUT IT Attorney Samuel G. Kling	2.00

CHESS & CHECKERS

__BEGINNER'S GUIDE TO WINNING CHESS Fred Reinfeld	2.00
__BETTER CHESS — How to Play Fred Reinfeld	2.00
__CHECKERS MADE EASY Tom Wiswell	2.00
__CHESS IN TEN EASY LESSONS Larry Evans	2.00
__CHESS MADE EASY Milton L. Hanauer	2.00
__CHESS MASTERY — A New Approach Fred Reinfeld	2.00
__CHESS PROBLEMS FOR BEGINNERS edited by Fred Reinfeld	2.00
__CHESS SECRETS REVEALED Fred Reinfeld	2.00

Melvin Powers
SELF-IMPROVEMENT
LIBRARY

Melvin Powers
SELF-IMPROVEMENT LIBRARY

HORSE PLAYERS' WINNING GUIDES

_BETTING HORSES TO WIN *Les Conklin*	2.00
_HOW TO PICK WINNING HORSES *Bob McKnight*	2.00
_HOW TO WIN AT THE RACES *Sam (The Genius) Lewin*	2.00
_HOW YOU CAN BEAT THE RACES *Jack Kavanagh*	2.00
_MAKING MONEY AT THE RACES *David Barr*	2.00
_PAYDAY AT THE RACES *Les Conklin*	2.00
_SMART HANDICAPPING MADE EASY *William Bauman*	2.00

HYPNOTISM

_ADVANCED TECHNIQUES OF HYPNOSIS *Melvin Powers*	1.00
_CHILDBIRTH WITH HYPNOSIS *William S. Kroger, M.D.*	2.00
_HOW TO SOLVE YOUR SEX PROBLEMS WITH SELF-HYPNOSIS *Frank S. Caprio, M.D.*	2.00
_HOW TO STOP SMOKING THRU SELF-HYPNOSIS *Leslie M. LeCron*	2.00
_HOW TO USE AUTO-SUGGESTION EFFECTIVELY *John Duckworth*	2.00
_HOW YOU CAN BOWL BETTER USING SELF-HYPNOSIS *Jack Heise*	2.00
_HOW YOU CAN PLAY BETTER GOLF USING SELF-HYPNOSIS *Heise*	2.00
_HYPNOSIS AND SELF-HYPNOSIS *Bernard Hollander, M.D.*	2.00
_HYPNOTISM *(Originally published in 1893) Carl Sextus*	3.00
_HYPNOTISM & PSYCHIC PHENOMENA *Simeon Edmunds*	2.00
_HYPNOTISM MADE EASY *Dr. Ralph Winn*	2.00
_HYPNOTISM MADE PRACTICAL *Louis Orton*	2.00
_HYPNOTISM REVEALED *Melvin Powers*	1.00
_HYPNOTISM TODAY *Leslie LeCron & Jean Bordeaux, Ph.D.*	2.00
_MEDICAL HYPNOSIS HANDBOOK *Drs. Van Pelt, Ambrose, Newbold*	2.00
_MODERN HYPNOSIS *Lesley Kuhn & Salvatore Russo, Ph.D.*	3.00
_NEW CONCEPTS OF HYPNOSIS *Bernard C. Gindes, M.D.*	3.00
_POST-HYPNOTIC INSTRUCTIONS *Arnold Furst*	2.00
How to give post-hypnotic suggestions for therapeutic purposes.	
_PRACTICAL GUIDE TO SELF-HYPNOSIS *Melvin Powers*	2.00
_PRACTICAL HYPNOTISM *Philip Magonet, M.D.*	1.00
_SECRETS OF HYPNOTISM *S. J. Van Pelt, M.D.*	2.00
_SELF-HYPNOSIS *Paul Adams*	2.00
_SELF-HYPNOSIS Its Theory, Technique & Application *Melvin Powers*	2.00
_SELF-HYPNOSIS A Conditioned-Response Technique *Laurance Sparks*	3.00
_THERAPY THROUGH HYPNOSIS *edited by Raphael H. Rhodes*	3.00

JUDAICA

_HOW TO LIVE A RICHER & FULLER LIFE *Rabbi Edgar F. Magnin*	2.00
_MODERN ISRAEL *Lily Edelman*	2.00
_OUR JEWISH HERITAGE *Rabbi Alfred Wolf & Joseph Gaer*	2.00
_ROMANCE OF HASSIDISM *Jacob S. Minkin*	2.50
_SERVICE OF THE HEART *Evelyn Garfield, Ph.D.*	3.00
_STORY OF ISRAEL IN COINS *Jean & Maurice Gould*	2.00
_STORY OF ISRAEL IN STAMPS *Maxim & Gabriel Shamir*	1.00
_TONGUE OF THE PROPHETS *Robert St. John*	3.00
_TREASURY OF COMFORT *edited by Rabbi Sidney Greenberg*	3.00

MARRIAGE, SEX & PARENTHOOD

METAPHYSICS & OCCULT

SELF-HELP & INSPIRATIONAL

___HOW TO ATTRACT GOOD LUCK A. H. Z. Carr   2.00
___HOW TO CONTROL YOUR DESTINY Norvell   2.00
___HOW TO DEVELOP A WINNING PERSONALITY Martin Panzer   2.00
___HOW TO DEVELOP AN EXCEPTIONAL MEMORY Young & Gibson   3.00
___HOW TO OVERCOME YOUR FEARS M. P. Leahy, M.D.   2.00
___HOW YOU CAN HAVE CONFIDENCE AND POWER Les Giblin   2.00
___I WILL Ben Sweetland   2.00
___LEFT-HANDED PEOPLE Michael Barsley   3.00
___MAGIC IN YOUR MIND U. S. Andersen   3.00
___MAGIC OF THINKING BIG Dr. David J. Schwartz   2.00
___MAGIC POWER OF YOUR MIND Walter M. Germain   3.00
___MENTAL POWER THRU SLEEP SUGGESTION Melvin Powers   1.00
___ORIENTAL SECRETS OF GRACEFUL LIVING Boye De Mente   1.00
___PRACTICAL GUIDE TO SUCCESS & POPULARITY C. W. Bailey   2.00
___PSYCHO-CYBERNETICS Maxwell Maltz, M.D.   2.00
___SECRET OF SECRETS U. S. Andersen   3.00
___STUTTERING AND WHAT YOU CAN DO ABOUT IT W. Johnson, Ph.D.   2.00
___SUCCESS-CYBERNETICS U. S. Andersen   2.00
___10 DAYS TO A GREAT NEW LIFE William E. Edwards   2.00
___THINK AND GROW RICH Napoleon Hill   3.00
___THREE MAGIC WORDS U. S. Andersen   3.00
___TREASURY OF THE ART OF LIVING Sidney S. Greenberg   3.00
___YOU ARE NOT THE TARGET Laura Huxley   3.00
___YOUR SUBCONSCIOUS POWER Charles M. Simmons   3.00

SPORTS

___ARCHERY — An Expert's Guide Don Stamp   2.00
___BICYCLING FOR FUN AND GOOD HEALTH Kenneth E. Luther   2.00
___CAMPING-OUT 101 Ideas & Activities Bruno Knobel   2.00
___COMPLETE GUIDE TO FISHING Vlad Evanoff   2.00
___HOW TO WIN AT POCKET BILLIARDS Edward D. Knuchell   3.00
___MOTORCYCLING FOR BEGINNERS I. G. Edmonds   2.00
___PRACTICAL BOATING W. S. Kals   3.00
___SECRET OF BOWLING STRIKES Dawson Taylor   2.00
___SECRET OF PERFECT PUTTING Horton Smith & Dawson Taylor   2.00
___SECRET WHY FISH BITE James Westman   2.00
___SKIER'S POCKET BOOK Otti Wiedman (4¼" x 6")   2.50
___TABLE TENNIS MADE EASY Johnny Leach   2.00

TENNIS LOVERS' LIBRARY

___BEGINNER'S GUIDE TO WINNING TENNIS Helen Hull Jacobs   2.00
___HOW TO BEAT BETTER TENNIS PLAYERS Loring Fiske   3.00
___HOW TO IMPROVE YOUR TENNIS—Style, Strategy & Analysis C. Wilson   2.00
___PSYCH YOURSELF TO BETTER TENNIS Dr. Walter A. Luszki   2.00
___TENNIS FOR BEGINNERS Dr. H. A. Murray   2.00
___TENNIS MADE EASY Joel Brecheen   2.00
___WEEKEND TENNIS—How to have fun & win at the same time Bill Talbert   2.00

WILSHIRE MINIATURE LIBRARY (4¼" x 6" in full color)

___BUTTERFLIES   2.50
___INTRODUCTION TO MINERALS   2.50
___LIPIZZANERS & THE SPANISH RIDING SCHOOL   2.50
___PRECIOUS STONES AND PEARLS   2.50
___SKIER'S POCKET BOOK   2.50

WILSHIRE PET LIBRARY

___DOG TRAINING MADE EASY & FUN John W. Kellogg   2.00
___HOW TO RAISE & TRAIN YOUR PUPPY Jeff Griffen   2.00
___PIGEONS: HOW TO RAISE & TRAIN THEM William H. Allen, Jr.   2.00

PSYCHO-CYBERNETICS
A New Technique for Using Your Subconscious Power
by Maxwell Maltz, M.D., F.I.C.S.
Contents:
1. The Self Image: Your Key to a Better Life. 2. Discovering the Success Me anism Within You 3. Imagination—The First Key to Your Success Mechani 4. Dehypnotize Yourself from False Beliefs 5. How to Utilize the Power Rational Thinking 6. Relax and Let Your Success Mechanism Work for Y 7. You Can Acquire the Habit of Happiness 8. Ingredients of the Success-T Personality and How to Acquire Them 9. The Failure Mechanism: How to Ma It Work For You Instead of Against You 10. How to Remove Emotional Sca or How to Give Yourself an Emotional Face Lift 11. How to Unlock Your R Personality 12. Do-It-Yourself Tranquilizers That Bring Peace of Mind 13. H to Turn a Crisis into a Creative Opportunity.   **268 Pages . . .**

A PRACTICAL GUIDE TO SELF-HYPNOSIS
by Melvin Powers
Contents:
1. What You Should Know About Self-Hypnosis 2. What About the Dangers Hypnosis? 3. Is Hypnosis the Answer? 4. How Does Self-Hypnosis Work? 5. H to Arouse Yourself From the Self-Hypnotic State 6. How to Attain Self-Hy nosis 7. Deepening the Self-Hypnotic State 8. What You Should Know Abo Becoming an Excellent Subject 9. Techniques for Reaching the Somnambulis State. 10. A New Approach to Self-Hypnosis When All Else Fails 11. Psycl logical Aids and Their Function 12. The Nature of Hypnosis   **120 Pages . . .**

A GUIDE TO RATIONAL LIVING
by Albert Ellis, Ph.D. & Robert A. Harper, Ph.D.
Contents:
1. How Far Can You Go With Self-Analysis? 2. You Feel as You Think 3. Fe ing Well by Thinking Straight 4. What Your Feelings Really Are 5. Thin ing Yourself Out of Emotional Disturbances 6. Recognizing and Attacki Neurotic Behavior 7. Overcoming the Influences of the Past 8. How Reasona is Reason? 9. The Art of Never Being Desperately Unhappy 10. Tackling Di Needs for Approval 11. Eradicating Dire Fears of Failure 12. How to St Blaming and Start Living 13. How to Be Happy Though Frustrated 14. Cc trolling Your Own Destiny 15. Conquering Anxiety 16. Conquering Self-d cipline 17. Rewriting Your Personal History 18. Accepting Reality 19. Ove coming Inertia and Becoming Creatively Absorbed   **208 Pages . . .**

A GUIDE TO SUCCESSFUL MARRIAGE
by Albert Ellis, Ph.D. & Robert A. Harper, Ph.D.
Contents:
1. Modern Marriage: Hotbed of Neurosis 2. Factors Causing Marital Distur ance 3. Gauging Marital Compatibility 4. Problem Solving in Marriage 5. C We Be Intelligent About Marriage? 6. Love or Infatuation? 7. To Marry or N To Marry 8. Sexual Preparation for Marriage 9. Impotence in the Male 10. Fr gidity in the Female 11. Sex "Excess" 12. Controlling Sex Impulses 13. No monogamous Desires 14. Communication in Marriage 15. Children 16. In-la 17. Marital Incompatibility Versus Neurosis 18. Divorce 19. Succeeding in Ma riage 20. Selected Readings   **304 Pages . . . $**

HOW YOU CAN HAVE CONFIDENCE & POWER
by Les Giblin
Contents:
1. Your Key to Success and Happiness 2. How to Use the Basic Secret for I fluencing Others 3. How to Cash in on Your Hidden Assets 4. How to Contr the Actions & Attitudes of Others 5. How You Can Create a Good Impressi on Other People 6. Techniques for Making & Keeping Friends 7. How to U Three Big Secrets for Attracting People 8. How to Make the Other Person F Friendly—Instantly 9. How You Can Develop Skill in Using Words 10. T Technique of "White Magic" 11. How to Get Others to See Things Your Way Quickly 12. A Simple, Effective Plan of Action That Will Bring You Succe and Happiness.   **180 Pages . . .**